WEAVING PRAYER INTO YOUR LIFE

WEAVING PRAYER INTO YOUR LIFE

*Daily Prayer for
Orthodox Christians*

By

Robert J. Peterson

Fairway Press
Lima, Ohio

Weaving Prayer Into Your Life

FIRST EDITION
Copyright @ 2019 by
Robert J. Peterson

All rights reserved. No portion of this book may be reproduced or utilized in any form or by any means, electronic or mechanical including photocopying, without permission in writing from the author. Inquiries should be addressed to: Robert J. Peterson, 114 Foster Center Road, Foster, RI 02825 or email: peterson20@cox.net.

Library of Congress Control Number: 2019902821

ISBN-13: 978-0-7880-2974-5
ISBN-10: 0-7880-2974-6

PRINTED IN USA

This book is dedicated to

Father Nick Milas

and

the people of

Holy Trinity Greek Orthodox Church

Danielson, Connecticut

who so graciously received us

into the

Orthodox Church

Preface

This book is an attempt by one, who came to Orthodoxy late in life, to find a way to pray daily. We live in a modern culture and speak American English as a primary, and for many our only, language. As many of my Greek-speaking friends know, only too well, one reverts to a person's birth language when one prays.

The level of English used in this book avoids the slang of the American street, but is an attempt to use vocabulary or style recognizable by a person with a high school education. The vocabulary and style of the prayers ought to point us to God, and not to the material itself. Orthodox liturgy is beautiful, but it is not primarily an art form. It is the worship of God.

This book is for an Orthodox family or individual, living in the world and making a living in the rough and tumble of commercial life. It contains both traditional prayers, and prayers pointing to contemporary life. The focus is the teaching of Scripture and the theology of the Orthodox Church. It is presumed that the person using this book will be a part of a parish, and will participate in the worship and sacraments of that parish. This is not from the monastery, nor is it monastic light. The wonderful contributions of the monastery need to be recognized and valued, and form much of our approach to prayer in Orthodoxy.

The point of this book is to offer each day to the Lord, through Scripture and prayer. It is important to keep in mind that the purpose of prayer is to allow the Holy Spirit to form us into the persons and souls God desires (theosis): "Therefore you shall be perfect, just as your Father in heaven is perfect" (Matthew 5:48 OSB).

The author is indebted to Fr. Theodore Stylianopoulos, Th.D. who graciously read this manuscript and offered many helpful corrections and suggestions. I am also indebted to my wife, Martha, who spent many hours making corrections and keeping me focused on what is important.

Contents

Preface	7
The Way of Prayer	11
Morning Prayer	17
Evening Prayer	55
The Symbol of Faith	89
Prayers of Commemoration	91
Table Prayers	103
Abbreviations	107
Daily Bible Readings -- Year I	111
Daily Bible Readings -- Year II	149
Sources and Acknowledgments	189

The Way of Prayer

As a child, I was encouraged to pray and read the Bible every day. I was taught the Lord's Prayer and a child's night time prayer, but not much more. Later, I tried reading the Bible but had no real plan for reading it, so I got to the "begats" and set it aside. I heard many a sermon on prayer and was told about the blessings of prayer and the kinds of prayer, but no one gave me a plan for prayer that would apply to an ordinary person living in our modern society.

Before being received into Orthodoxy, I tried many methods of prayer. Some were just too simple or repetitious. Daily prayer for an individual or a family is not the same as the vocation of prayer we see in the monastery. While the blessings of the monastery have overflowed to the benefit of us all, daily prayer for the ordinary person is not simply a shorter form of monastic prayer.

To find the blessings and benefits of prayer, one must first begin with a certain mindset. Prayer is much more like physical conditioning than winning the lottery. There is no instant muscle. Muscle in the human body must be built up by conditioning on a regular basis. Likewise, the conditioning of the soul comes from setting aside a time to pray. A soul like a healthy body is built day by day.

In our American society, we stress the physical (exercise and diet); and we stress education, almost as if education will save us and deliver heaven on earth. However, our society overlooks the soul of a person. Our political leaders stress the physical, and constantly talk about education, but the soul is relegated to the privacy of the individual, and too often is ignored.

To grow as a Christian and seek to be more and more Christlike, we need to cultivate a life of worship and prayer. We live in a society that values freedom but does not value becoming Christlike. We can rejoice that we have the freedom to worship God and serve him -- but drawing closer to Christ in worship and prayer is up to us.

There are times in life when we feel closer to God. It may be a mountain top experience where all the energies and beauty of nature surround us and we feel that we can almost reach out to God himself. There are also times in life when God seems so far away. Life seems to overwhelm us, and in sorrow or pain we feel deserted. Most of the time, we go about our lives thinking more about our daily living than the presence of God.

The discipline of prayer is the way Christians personally enter into the story of the covenant -- the story of God dealing with us to draw us to himself. The understanding of who we are and how we are to see the world around us begins with our spiritual father, Abraham, and finds its culmination in the person of Jesus Christ, God come to us.

Daily prayer for the Christian is not a substitute for the Church. Christians are bound together in the church, which is the very body of Christ. Personal daily prayer is no substitute for the divine liturgy, the sacraments, and the beautiful worship within the church itself. Daily prayer is a complement to the Liturgy, and is a part of the process of becoming more and more Christlike (*theosis*). Please remember that the main purpose of prayer is to lead us to do the will of God, not to have God give us what we want.

A Time for Prayer

The first step in daily prayer is to set aside each day a time for prayer. Many find that a time in the morning as one arises from sleep, and sometime before bed, is a way to begin the day and end the day with prayer. In a family with small children, the adults may want to pray together without the children but incorporate some of the daily prayers with the meals, perhaps reading a psalm along with table prayers. A family with older children could offer evening prayer together after the evening meal. The important point is to make time for prayer as a regular part of life, especially family life.

Beginning With Three Things

Orthodox prayer is a beautiful garden with many flowers, but daily prayer normally begins with three basic things: a Bible, the church calendar, and a plan. This may sound neither spiritual nor inspirational, but it is a simple and sensible starting point. With a basic outline of daily prayer, we will have a way to pray without "reinventing the wheel" each day. The Bible, especially the psalms, is the prayer book of the church. Most parishes provide a liturgical calendar giving readings, saint's days, and the dates for the seasons of worship.

The Holy Scriptures

The center of individual prayer is the Bible readings. The psalms are the primary prayers of the Bible. They are beautiful literature, and they lead us through all the "ups and downs" of life. However, the psalms are not read as literature, but as food for our souls, helping us grow and be shaped by God's presence. The psalms form a large part of our Orthodox liturgy. On page 9, there are suggested opening psalms for each morning, and on page 47, Psalm 50(51) the opening psalm for evening prayer. If you read the psalms listed in the Daily Lectionaries (p. 70 ff), one in the morning and one in the evening, you will read through the Psalms regularly throughout the year.

There is a difference between the numbering of the Psalms in the Septuagint (the Greek translation) and the Masoritic (the Hebrew) editions. You will see, in this book, psalms numbered with one number in parentheses.

The number without the parenthesis follows the Greek numbering system, while the number in parentheses follows the Hebrew numbering system.

There are many translations of the Bible on the market. Some are better than others. There is a difference among the groups that use the Old Testament, such as The Orthodox, the Roman Catholic, and the Protestant groups. Each has a slightly different list of books for the Old Testament. (*see p. xiii of the Orthodox Study Bible, for the three lists.*) Please consult your priest or pastor to get his advice in choosing a Bible for prayer. There are many translations which may or may not be helpful.

The readings from the Old Testament, Epistles, and Gospels can be arranged in several ways. The calendar published by the Archdiocese, which most parishes provide to the people, has listed in it readings for each day. Using these readings, we read the lessons used in the liturgy of the whole Church, on that day. These readings can also be found at the Archdiocese website goarch.com, and in the lectionary printed in the back of the *Orthodox Study Bible*, pp.1767-1774

A second method is to use the daily lectionaries included with this book. If you follow these lectionaries, you will read through most of the Old Testament in two years, and you will read through all of the New Testament each year. One of the advantages of this plan is that you will read the books of the Bible page by page and section by section, so that you will begin to know the full story of each section, gospel, or letter. If you have never read the Bible completely, this is a good way to start that reading.

A third method of reading the Bible is to use the Orthodox reading plan (found at www.holycrosshermitagepa.org/files/Bible-Reading-Plan.pdf).

Four ribbons of different colors make it easy to find the four parts of the Bible commonly used in daily prayer: Old Testament readings, the Psalms, the Epistles, and the Gospels.

It is important to eventually choose some method of reading the Bible daily. The point is that, to shape our souls, we need to let the stories and teachings of Holy Scripture so enter our consciousness that we can "pray without ceasing."

A Plan for Daily Prayer

When people speak of a "rule of prayer," they normally mean a plan or method for offering prayer on a regular basis. This is similar to having a "workout schedule" for physical conditioning. Just as there is no final or perfect workout plan for exercise, there is not one perfect way to offer prayer. However, some plan is necessary.

A plan for daily prayer should include the following:

> Opening Prayer or Prayers
> A Psalm or Psalms
> Scripture Reading or Readings
> Prayers (Intercessions and Thanksgivings)
> Concluding Prayer or Prayers

Each person or family needs to find a way to build a plan that will work for them. Listed on pp. 165-166 f. there are books on prayer. You may find these books to be a very valuable resource for offering prayer and finding resources for prayer.

A Suggested Plan

Beginning on p. 17 ff., this book suggests a plan for Morning and Evening Prayer. It follows the outline of Opening Prayers, Psalms and Readings, Prayers of Intercession and Thanksgiving, and Concluding Prayers. The outlines for Morning Prayer (see p.17) and Evening Prayer (see p. 45) have these sections clearly marked. Using this plan will take about 12 to 15 minutes for Morning Prayer and about the same time for Evening Prayer. This is the rule of prayer the author uses daily.

The opening prayers come from the opening of the Orthodox service of Matins or Vespers. In this way our individual prayer is set within the context of the prayers of the Church.

Suggested Psalms and Scripture readings can be found in the Lectionaries on pp. 93 ff.

The third part of daily prayer is offering prayers of intercession and thanksgiving. As examples of these prayers, there are six things for which to pray included in Morning Prayer, and six things for which to give thanks in Evening Prayer. There is a set for each day of the week. In addition, there is a set of prayers for commemorating the seasons of the Liturgy and the Saints of the Orthodox Church on p. 73 ff. Offering these prayers is a very good start in learning how to pray and learning those things for which we are to pray.

The concluding prayers are taken from the conclusion of Matins and Vespers, and are adapted to this format.

Certainly, you can adapt this plan for your own purposes or needs. Schedules vary, and families have many time constraints.

The habit of prayer and the blessings of prayer do not come easily. At times, we forget. At times, we just do not feel like it. We are human. However, the best part is that we can start again and stay on the road our Lord sets before us.

Morning Prayer

Arising from sleep and before the duties of the day, if possible, stand before the icons and offer the day to Christ. Make the sign of the cross and say:

Opening Prayers

In the name of Father and the Son and the Holy Spirit Amen.

Glory to you, our God; glory to you.

Heavenly King, Comforter, the Spirit of truth, who is present everywhere filling all things, Treasury of good things and Giver of life, come and dwell in us. Cleanse us of every stain, and save our souls, gracious Lord.

Holy God, Holy Mighty, Holy Immortal, have mercy on us (3).

Glory to the Father and the Son and the Holy Spirit, now and forever and to the ages of the ages. Amen.

All-holy Trinity, have mercy on us. Lord, forgive our sins. Master, pardon our transgressions. Holy One, visit and heal our infirmities for your name's sake.

Lord, have mercy.
Lord, have mercy.
Lord, have mercy.

Glory to the Father and the Son and the Holy Spirit, now and forever and to the ages of ages. Amen.

Our Father, who art in heaven, hallowed be thy name. Thy kingdom come. Thy will be done on earth as it is in heaven. Give us this day our daily bread, and forgive us our trespasses as we forgive those who trespass against us. And lead us not into temptation, but deliver us from evil.

For yours is the kingdom and the power and the glory, of the Father and the Son and the Holy Spirit, now and forever and to the ages of ages. Amen.

Lord God, our heavenly Father, you have brought us safely to this new day. Preserve us with your almighty power so that we may not fall into any sin nor be overtaken in temptation. Help and direct us in all we do, so we may fulfill your holy purposes. With the prayers of the *Theotokos*, have mercy on us. Amen.

Psalms and Readings

Morning Psalms

Here may be read the opening psalm. There is an opening psalm for each day of the week.

Sunday - Psalm 83(84)

*How lovely is thy dwelling place,
O Lord of hosts!!
My soul longs, yea, faints,
for the courts of the lord;
my heart and flesh sing for joy
to the living God.
Even the sparrow finds a home,
and the swallow a nest for herself,
where she may lay her young,
at thy altars, O Lord of hosts,
my King and my God.
Blessed are those who dwell in thy house,
ever singing thy praise!
Blessed are the men whose strength
is in thee,
in whose heart are the highways
to Zion.
As they go through the valley of Baca,
they make it a place of springs;
the early rain also covers it with pools.
They go from strength to strength;
the God of gods will be seen in Zion.
O Lord God of hosts, hear my prayer;
give ear, O God of Jacob!
Behold our shield, O God;
look upon the face of thine anointed!*

For a day in thy courts is better
than a thousand elsewhere.
I would rather be a doorkeeper in
the house of my God
than dwell in the tents of wickedness.
For the Lord God is a sun and shield;
he bestows favor and honor.
No good thing does the Lord withhold
from those who walk uprightly,
O Lord of hosts,
blessed is the man who trusts in thee!

Monday - Psalm 61(62)

For God alone my soul waits in silence;
from him comes my salvation.
He only is my rock and my salvation,
my fortress; I shall not be greatly moved.
How long will you set upon a man to shatter him,
all of you.
Like a leaning wall, a tottering fence?
They only plan to thrust him down from his
eminence.
They take pleasure in falsehood.
They bless with their mouths,
but inwardly they curse.
For God alone my soul waits in silence,
for my hope is from him.
He only is my rock and my salvation,
my fortress; I shall not be shaken.
On God rests my deliverance and my honor;
my mighty rock, my refuge is God.
Trust in him at all times, O people;
pour out your heart before him;
God is a refuge for us.
Men of low estate are but a breath,

men of high estate are a delusion;
in the balances they go up;
they are together lighter than a breath,
Put no confidence in extortion,
set no vain hopes on robbery;
if riches increase, set not your heart on them.
Once God has spoken;
twice have I heard this:
that power belongs to God;
and that to thee, O Lord, belongs steadfast love.
For thou dost requite a man according to his work.

Tuesday - Psalm 94(95)

O come, let us sing to the Lord;
let us make a joyful noise to the rock of our
salvation!
Let us come into his presence with thanksgiving;
let us make a joyful noise to him with songs of
praise!
For the Lord is a great God,
and a great King above all gods.
In his hand are the depths of the earth;
the heights of the mountains are his also.
The sea is his, for he made it;
for his hands formed the dry land.
O come, let us worship and bow down,
let us kneel before the Lord, our Maker!
For he is our God,
and we are the people of his pasture,
and the sheep of his hand.
O that today you would hearken to his voice!
Harden not your hearts, as at Meribah,
as on the day at Massah in the wilderness,
when your fathers tested me,

and put me to the proof, though they had
seen my work.
For forty years I loathed that generation and said,
"They are a people who err in heart,
and they do not regard my ways."
Therefore I swore in my anger
that they should not enter my rest.

Wednesday - Psalm 8

O Lord, our Lord,
how majestic is thy name in all the earth!
Thou whose glory above the heavens is chanted
by the mouths of babes and infants,
thou hast founded a bulwark because of thy foes,
to still the enemy and the avenger.
When I look at thy heavens, the work of thy
fingers, the moon and the stars which thou
hast established;
what is man that thou art mindful of him,
and the son of man that thou dost
care for him?
Yet thou hast made him little less than God;
and dost crown him with glory and honor.
Thou hast given him dominion over
the works of thy hands;
thou hast put all things under his feet,
all sheep and oxen,
and also the beasts of the field,
the birds of the air, and the fish of the sea,
whatever passes along the paths of the sea.
O Lord, our Lord,
how majestic is thy name in all the earth!

Thursday - Psalm 120(121)

I lift up my eyes to the hills.
From whence does my help come?
My help comes from the Lord,
who made heaven and earth.
He will not let your foot be moved;
he who keeps you will not slumber.
Behold, He who keeps Israel
will neither slumber nor sleep.
The Lord is your keeper;
the Lord is your shade on your right hand.
The sun shall not smite you by day
nor the moon by night.
The Lord will keep you from all evil;
he will keep your life.
The Lord will keep your going out
and your coming in from this time forth and for evermore.

Friday - Psalm 62(63)

O God, thou art my God, I seek thee,
my soul thirsts for thee;
my flesh faints for thee,
as in a dry and weary land where no water is.
So I have looked upon thee in the sanctuary,
beholding thy power and glory.
Because thy steadfast love is better than life,
my lips will praise thee.
So I will bless thee as long as I live;
I will lift up my hands and call on thy name.
My soul is feasted as with marrow and fat,
and my mouth praises thee with joyful lips,
when I think of thee upon my bed,
and meditate on thee in the watches of the night;
for thou hast been my help,

and in the shadow of thy wings I sing for joy.
My soul clings to thee;
thy right hand upholds me.
But those who seek to destroy my life
shall go down into the depths of the earth;
they shall be given over to the power of the sword,
they shall be prey for jackals.
But the king shall rejoice in God;
all who swear by him shall glory;
for the mouths of liars will be stopped.

Saturday - Psalm 89(90)

Lord, thou hast been our dwelling place
in all generations.
Before the mountains were brought forth,
or ever thou hadst formed the earth
and the world, from everlasting to everlasting thou art God.
Thou turnest man back to the dust,
and sayest, "Turn back, O children of men!"
For a thousand years in thy sight
are but as yesterday when it is past,
or as a watch in the night.
Thou dost sweep men away; they are like a dream,
like grass which is renewed in the morning:
in the morning it flourishes and is renewed;
in the evening it fades and withers.
For we are consumed by thy anger;
by thy wrath we are overwhelmed.
Thou hast set our iniquities before thee,
our secret sins in the light of thy countenance.
For all our days pass away under thy wrath,
our years come to an end like a sigh.
The years of our life are threescore and ten,
or even by reason of strength fourscore;

yet their span is but toil and trouble;
they are soon gone, and we fly away.
Who considers the power of thy anger,
and thy wrath according to the fear of thee?
So teach us to number our days
that we may get a heart of wisdom.
Return, O Lord! How long?
Have pity on thy servants!
Satisfy us in the morning with thy steadfast love,
that we may rejoice and be glad all our days.
Make us glad as many days as thou hast afflicted us,
and as many years as we have seen evil.
Let thy work be manifest to thy servants,
and thy glorious power to their children.
Let the favor of the Lord our God be upon us,
and establish thou the work of our hands upon us,
yea, the work of our hands establish thou it.

Scripture Readings

It is most helpful for the development of our souls to read the Holy Scriptures on a daily basis. See p. 13 ff. for suggestions for reading the Scriptures daily.

The Creed (if not recited in Evening Prayer)

It is customary to recite the Nicene Creed each day (see p. 71). One normal place to recite the Creed is immediately after the reading of the Holy Scriptures, since the Creed summarizes the basic teaching of the Church.

Prayers of Intercession

The following is a set of six suggested intercessions for each day of the week. These prayers may be used as written; they may be used in part; they may be used as suggestions for silent prayer; or they may be combined with other intercessions and thanksgivings.

Sunday

Theme: The glory of God and his love for us
Intercessions: Sunday Morning

On this day, as we remember the resurrection of our Lord Jesus Christ from the dead, we give glory to your name, O God, for the gift of salvation and the love we have received from him.

Let us pray for:

1. The Church of Jesus Christ throughout the world, its people, its leaders, and its mission.

   Your grace abounds for all to see, Lord; and through your grace, you call us to be your Church. We pray for the Church of Jesus Christ, and for our bishops and priests who minister in his name, preaching the Word and administering the Sacraments. We pray for all who serve in your name. May we who bear the sign of Baptism reflect the person of Christ in our human relationships. Amen.

2. Our nation, our political leaders, and all who exercise authority.

   In your wisdom Lord, you have given us nations, authorities, and leaders. We pray for those who govern us that they may serve with justice, mercy, and wisdom. Help us to respect those in authority, and let those in authority be humble in all their dealings, knowing that no authority can stand outside of your divine will. Amen.

3. All people in all nations, for their welfare and for all who serve the common good.

   We remember the nations of the earth and people who -- like us -- yearn for peace, love, and hope. Lord, we pray for others; and where our vision is dim, and our hearts are small, lead us to continue to pray that we may see people as you see them, and love others as you would have us do. Lead us to serve and to support those who serve the welfare of all your people. Amen.

4. Our local civic community, our friends and neighbors, and all who help to make this a happy and safe place.

   In your wisdom, Father, you have given us the capacity to form friendships, to love neighbors, and to find human fulfillment -- living in community, one with another. We pray for those who guard our community, those who labor to keep it a healthy, safe, and beautiful place. Lead us to fulfill your divine intention for this place, and for the many people knit together within it. Amen.

5. Those who are sick; the troubled; and those who are in need.

   Lord God, you are our great physician, and you help us through those who practice the healing arts. We pray for the sick, the troubled, and those who need care. Guide those who minister to them; and lead us to be, more fully, your hands of healing and hope. Amen.

6. Our own lives, that we may walk with Jesus Christ this week and be a witness to his love for all.

Each step in our life is precious to you, O God; and no sparrow can fall without your notice. We ask you to guide us each day. Keep us away from temptation, and guard us lest we succumb to the evil around us. Lord God, help us walk with your Son, Jesus Christ, measuring our steps by his, that we may show his love and be his witnesses for all to see. Amen.

Monday

Theme: Creation and providence

Intercessions: Monday Morning

Almighty God, we praise you for all creation and the gift of life you have given us. In our Lord Jesus Christ, you have revealed your purposes for creation, and in him you have called us to live responsibly here on earth.

Let us pray for:

1. The nations of the earth.

   Lord God, you are the true king of all nations, and through your grace all that we enjoy exists. We pray for nations, governments, leaders, and peoples, so that -- seeking your justice, learning your word, and showing your love -- we, the families of the earth, may live in peace and harmony. Help us all to honor and respect the accomplishments, the good works, and the true value of all peoples. Amen.

2. Our own nation.

   Lord God, you have given us nations and governments for our common good. We pray for our own nation that you will lead us to seek truth and justice; mercy and compassion. Let your Spirit move upon us, that our endeavors may promote the common good, reflect the highest ideals, and lead this nation to peace and tranquility. Amen.

3. Our president.

   Send your Spirit, O God, upon (Name), the president of the United States, that *he* may have the knowledge, the will, and the strength to govern this people. Lead *him* in the exercise of *his* office that this nation will be well governed and led in the pursuit of peace and justice for all. Amen.

4. All who are in authority.

   Father, in your wisdom and in your love, you have placed leaders in authority over us. Help us to respect their offices, their judgments, and their labors on our behalf. Give us the ability to walk in humility, giving respect to whom respect is due, and honor to whom honor is due. We pray for all in authority that they will pursue their office in truth and justice, that your divine care may become manifest for all to see. Amen.

5. For peace in the world.

   Eternal God, you are the author of peace and goodwill among all people; so lead us in the ways of peace, so that -- as we seek the well-being of our neighbors, near and far -- your true peace will reign in our hearts, and we will learn to walk in your holy ways. Amen.

6. For harmony between people and races.

Lord God, your creative hand has given us the beauty of nature in its vast variety. We praise you for your providence which has given us races and peoples, and even the various gifts and talents which make human society possible. We pray for goodwill between and among peoples and races. Break down all false walls of division and enable us to love all your people with your divine love. Amen.

Tuesday

Theme: Revelation and human knowledge

Intercessions: Tuesday Morning

God our Father, you sent Jesus Christ, your Word, to reveal to us your truth, your gospel, and your love.

Let us pray for:

1. Our society.

    Lord God, you are the author of every good and perfect gift in life. We pray that we may use your gifts creatively and productively, so that our society will prosper and good things will be built among us. Remove from us that apathy toward life which dulls our appetite for excellence and causes us to shun those deeds of labor that will yield a healthy and happy community for all. Amen.

2. Those who labor, especially those who labor to make our lives easier.

    Lord God, each day we receive the help and labor of others. We accept the blessings of light and heat, food and clothing, and the many luxuries we enjoy; yet so often, we do not think of the people responsible for our comfort. We pray for those who labor; for those who give of themselves in arduous work and in creative tasks. Let your blessing be upon their hands and minds, and give us thankful hearts. Amen.

3. Leaders of business, industry, education, and human service.

   The diversity of life and the organization of society is a wonder to behold, O Lord. We pray for those who lead industry and organize business. We pray for those who develop and teach skills and make truth and knowledge available to many. We pray that you will bless them, and especially that you will bless those who serve human need and make life sweeter for all. Amen.

4. Those who maintain the security of society.

   Father, we pray for those who stand guard that we may be secure in our homes, free from the fear of anarchy, pillage and riot. We are grateful for police, for firefighters, those who answer emergency calls, and everyone who, like the good Samaritan, lifts hands where there is need. Amen.

5. The unemployed.

   Lord God, you have given us work to do on earth. You have called us to labor and to earn our living. We pray to you for those who desire work but cannot find it; for those who seek to be productive but find nothing to produce. Lord God, give them hope and confidence for the future -- and so inspire the leaders of business, industry, and society, that they will seek meaningful employment for every person with willing hands. Amen.

6. Those who are retired

    Lord God, send your blessing upon every person who is retired from a life of labor. Grant them a sense of fulfillment and accomplishment. Keep us mindful of their needs and of the great debt we owe to all who have passed on to us the good heritage we enjoy. Help us to be mindful of their needs and of the ways in which we can serve them as they have served us. Amen.

Wednesday

Theme: Reconciliation and Human Relationships
Intercessions: Wednesday Morning

Eternal God, in Jesus Christ you have reconciled us to yourself. Now let your Spirit sear our hearts with the meaning of the cross of Christ and enable us to apply the reconciling call of Christ to all of our relationships.

Let us pray for:

1. Our home and family.

   Father, in your love for us you have given us parents and children. The family is your first school of piety, of learning, and of morals. Defend and protect our homes and families that they may be fit instruments to do your will. In times when enemies lurk to destroy, send your Spirit to be our strong defense. Save us from every enemy of true love and of family devotion. Amen.

2. Children who have been deprived of homes.

   Lord God, we pray that you will open our hearts to children who have been deprived of homes or parents. Open our hearts to their circumstances and needs. Give us a lively interest in every group and agency of society that ministers to their wellbeing. Help us to have room in our hearts. Amen.

3. Our friends and relatives.

   In your wisdom, you have made us for each other -- and so much of the joy of life is found with friends and family members. We pray for the gift of friendship, that we may give friendship and receive it. Help us to be loyal to our friends and relatives, that in these relationships our greater relationship with you will shine forth. Amen.

4. The lonely, the rejected, and the despised.

   Lord Jesus Christ, you were the friend to the friendless; and no one who sought you in faith was turned away. We pray for all people -- especially the lonely, the rejected, and the despised. Move within our hearts that we may love as you have given example. Keep us mindful of the needs and longings of all your people. Amen.

5. Our relationships in daily life and work.

   Father, in our daily routine and in our sharing good things one with another, you give us joy and gladness. We pray for those around us who make our lives full. Assist us that we may bring joy and happiness; stability and understanding; to those around us. Let your Spirit, even through us, work a good work and bring your blessing to many. Amen.

6. Our enemies.

   Lord God, you did not intend enemies to exist upon this good earth. We know our distance from you when we see the hatred, enmity, and strife created between people. We pray for those who act as enemies. Let our hearts be changed, and lead us to that love and peace you intend for all. Amen.

Thursday

Theme: The Church of Jesus Christ

Intercessions: Thursday Morning

Eternal God, we glorify you because you have called us to be your people in Jesus Christ. We pray that your Church will be obedient and responsive to the call of our Lord.

Let us pray for:

1. The Church throughout the world.

    We pray for your one holy, catholic, and apostolic Church, O Lord, that we who are your people may be responsive in every way to your divine will. Give us a vision of the height, the depth, and the true meaning of your Church, so that we may be humble and see your Spirit calling people of every race, every nation, and every tribe, to your presence. Give us eyes to behold, O Lord. Amen.

2. Our own congregation and our fellow Christians.

    In your love and wisdom, O Lord, you have called us to be your people, bound together in congregations, for worship and praise. We pray for our congregation that we may be bold to declare your word, and to do your work in our place. Give us your Spirit of love and compassion, so that -- being brothers and sisters one to another -- each may know your divine presence in our midst. Amen.

3. The ministry of the Church and our own ministers.

   Lord God, through prophets and apostles you have spoken your word and have taught us your holy Gospel. We pray now for our bishops and priests whom you call to minister in your holy name -- teaching your word, administering your sacraments, and calling us to become mature in all faith and holiness. Give us the grace to follow our spiritual leaders as they minister in your name. Lead them in the ways of truth, following their Lord and our Lord, Jesus Christ the righteous. Amen.

4. The mission of the Church and our own missionaries.

   Father, you have sent us into your world to do your work and to preach the Gospel to all: to the rich and the poor; healthy or broken; free or slave. Quicken our hearts and enliven our thoughts that this mission you give us may be performed. We pray for our part of your work, and we pray for those we support in your name. *Especially now, do we remember* (Name) *and their work,* that you will guide them, support them, and lift them up. Amen.

5. The unity of the Church.

   Father, we confess before you our sins which have divided Christians over many centuries. As our Lord prayed to you that they all be one, so we pray for healing that we may be one holy, catholic, and apostolic Church. Heal our minds that we may love with the love of Christ; heal our wills that pride and ambition may be yielded to the Spirit of unity you desire in us. Make us whole. Amen.

6. The guidance of the Church by the Holy Spirit.

   Almighty God, in our blindness we so often seek to be something in our own strength, seeking even to build your Church. We pray now for strength -- the strength of your Spirit -- to flee the temptation to rely upon ourselves; and for the strength to wait upon His divine power. Guide us, direct us, and turn us again to your holy word, that in word and sacrament we may hear your truth and be mature members of your Church. Fill us with power from on high. Amen.

Friday

Theme: All that meets human need

Intercessions: Friday Morning

As Jesus Christ came not to be served but to serve and to give his life as a sacrifice for many, send us to serve and to bind up that which is broken in life.

Let us pray for:

1. The poor, the hungry, and the needy.

   Lord Jesus Christ, in your earthly life you taught us by word and by example to feed the hungry, to clothe the naked, and to give to those who cannot repay. Hold before us the needs of people and open our hearts to respond. We pray that we, being led by your Spirit, may become your hands and feet to do this work. Almighty God, move us to have your divine compassion. Amen.

2. Those who are refugees.

   There was no room for the birth of your Son, save a stable, and he was saved by a flight to Egypt. Lord God, we pray that we may have love and compassion for refugees, as you have -- for in Christ, you know their plight and despair. Help us to open our hearts, our homes, and our communities to those who have been deprived of their homes and driven from their lands. Amen.

3. Those who suffer persecution.

   Lord God, we humans -- by our sin, through our greed, and in our fear -- often harm one another in body and spirit. We have persecuted leaders and prophets, even the weak, the defenseless, and the powerless. We pray for those who are persecuted who are deprived of human freedoms and basic rights. Help us, by your Spirit, to stand with those who suffer persecution and so declare your love for every person. Amen.

4. Those who suffer because of our sins and the sins of others.

   Eternal God, the freedom you give us is frightening. So often we do not know how to use it, and we allow our greed, hatred, and lust to find an opportunity to control us. In our sin, we hurt people; and many suffer because of the sins of others. Father, reform us by your Spirit, and lift up those who suffer because of others' sins. Teach us how to repent and how to make true amendment for our sins. Amen.

5. Those who are victims of disasters and human carelessness.

   The ways of your universe are so often difficult to understand, and we cannot find reasons for the sufferings we experience. Help us to trust you in the difficult times. Send your Spirit of comfort to those who suffer from accidents, from carelessness, or from the forces of nature. Give us a heart of compassion that we may learn to share the sorrows as well as the good things of life. Amen.

6. Those who serve the physical and mental needs of other people.

   Lord, you are the great Great Physician -- healing our bodies, our minds, and our souls. We pray for those whom you use to do your work of healing. We pray for physicians and surgeons; for nurses and other specialists who stand guard to help us in times of sickness and distress. Teach us all to minister to one another, and so to learn to follow the example you gave us in Jesus Christ our Lord. Amen.

Saturday

Theme: The fulfillment of God's purposes

Intercessions: Saturday Morning

Holy Father, lead us to trust your eternal purposes, that resting in you we may know the peace which comes from a secure and eternal future.

Let us pray for:

1. All those who are tempted and in despair.

   We are so often led astray by the yearnings of our hearts. Within us is such a great capacity for darkness and evil. We pray, Father, for those who are wrestling with temptation. Assist them in their struggle, and help us to recognize temptation in our own lives. Lift us all from the depths of despair, and grant us the light and peace of your presence. Amen.

2. The sick and the handicapped.

   Lord God, we bring to you our weaknesses and our frailties, for you are the Author of life and the giver of health and healing. We pray for those who are sick, the troubled in body and mind. We pray for those who journey through life with heavy burdens. Father, we are assured of your goodness and your final triumph over all sickness, evil, and death -- yet while we await your final victory, help us to bear one another's burdens and so fulfill the law of Christ. Amen.

3. Those who mourn and are left alone.

   Death is our final enemy, and you have promised us that it will be destroyed. We pray now for those who experience the loneliness and sorrow caused by death. Send your Spirit of assurance to all lonely people that they may recognize their Lord walking with them in their hour of need. Help us to seek out the sorrowing, the lonely, and the neglected, that we may be your instruments of cheer and comfort. Amen.

4. Those who have little hope and weak faith.

   In our darkest moments, we turn to you, Father. Our faith is like a morning breeze or like the dew which goes quickly away. We pray not only for ourselves, that we will be delivered when hope fails and faith seems to fly away, but we also pray for all those who share such darkness with us. Preserve us, O Lord, and save us from utter despair that hope may be rekindled and faith be born anew. Grant every human the hope that sustains life and nourishes faith. Amen.

5. The enemies of Christ.

   Your mercy and forgiveness abound to all, and we marvel at the grace you give us in Jesus Christ. We pray for those who turn aside from him and spurn his name, and for those who are indifferent to him. When we, in our sin, bring discredit upon the name of Christ and prevent others from coming to him, chasten us, and help us amend our ways. Let us become fit instruments to reflect the gospel of your divine Son so that many a heart will be transformed. Amen.

6. The communion of saints

   Almighty God, you have joined together your people of every age into a holy communion; a divine fellowship of saints. As you draw us together, you fashion us into the mystical Body of Christ. Grant that we your people -- now, on earth -- may follow every good and virtuous act of all your saints so that we may bear true witness and boldly confess your name for all to hear. Then, in your mercy, lead us to that Church triumphant -- where we may share with all your people those unspeakable joys prepared for those who love you. Amen.

On Saturdays, it is appropriate to offer prayers for those who have fallen asleep in the Lord. (see: "Prayers of Commemoration," p. 73)

Here one may offer other prayers, personal prayers, or silent prayer.

Concluding Prayers

John, Baptizer of Christ, remember us, so that we may be saved from our sins. For to you has been given grace to intercede for us.

Holy apostles, and all you saints, intercede for us so that we may be saved from danger and sorrow. We have received you as fervent defenders before the Savior.

Theotokos, beneath your compassion we seek refuge. Do not overlook our prayers, but deliver us from danger, Only Pure and Blessed One.

My hope is the Father; my refuge, the Son; my protection, the Holy Spirit. Holy Trinity, glory to you.

Through the prayers of our holy fathers, Lord Jesus Christ our God, have mercy and save us. Amen.

Evening Prayer

Evening prayer may be offered at the end of the day, with the family after the evening meal, or before retiring.

Opening Prayers

In the name of Father and the Son and the Holy Spirit. Amen.

Glory to you, our God; glory to you.

Heavenly King, Comforter, the Spirit of truth, who are present everywhere filling all things, treasury of good things and giver of life, come and dwell in us. Cleanse us of every stain, and save our souls, gracious Lord.

Holy God, Holy Mighty, Holy Immortal, have mercy on us (3).

Glory to the Father and the Son and the Holy Spirit, now and forever and to the ages of ages. Amen.

All-holy Trinity, have mercy on us. Lord, forgive our sins. Master, pardon our transgressions. Holy One, visit and heal our infirmities for your name's sake.

Lord, have mercy.
Lord, have mercy.
Lord, have mercy.

Glory to the Father and the Son and the Holy Spirit, now and forever and to the ages of ages. Amen.

Our Father, who art in heaven, hallowed be thy name. Thy kingdom come; thy will be done on earth as it is in heaven. Give us this day our daily bread, and forgive us our trespasses as we forgive those who trespass against us. And lead us not into temptation, but deliver us from evil.

For Yours is the kingdom and the power and the glory -- of the Father and the Son and the Holy Spirit -- now and forever and to the ages of ages. Amen.

Eternal Father, you are the source of everything that is good and holy. Forgive us when we stray from your path and when we turn to selfish ways and sinful thoughts. Let our lives again follow Jesus Christ, our life and hope. Defend us from every peril and danger of this night and grant us that peace which the world cannot give. With the prayers of the *Theotokos*, have mercy on us. Amen.

Psalms and Readings

Evening Psalms

Here may be read Psalm 50(51)) and/or the psalms suggested in the section on Daily Bible Readings.

Psalm 50(51)

An Evening Confession

Have mercy on me, O God, according to your great mercy;
> according to the multitude of your compassion
> blot out my transgressions.

Wash me thoroughly from my iniquity
> and cleanse me from my sin!

For I know my transgressions
> and my sin is ever before me.

Against you, you only, have I sinned
> and done that which is evil in your sight; so
> that you are justified in your sentence
> and blameless in your judgment.

Behold, I was brought forth in iniquity,
> and in sin did my mother bear me.

Behold, you desire truth;
You manifested to me the secret and
> hidden things of your wisdom.

You will sprinkle me with hyssop
> and I shall be clean;

You will wash me, and I shall be made whiter than
> snow.

You will let me hear joy and gladness;
> the afflicted bones will rejoice.

Hide your face from my sins
> and blot out all my iniquities.

Create in me a clean heart, O God,
    and put a new and right spirit within me.
Cast me not away from your presence,
    and take not your Holy Spirit from me.
Restore to me the joy of your salvation
    and establish me with your directing Spirit.

Assurance of Forgiveness

Then I will teach transgressors your ways and ungodly men will turn to you.

Deliver me from bloodguiltiness, O God, the God of my salvation, and my tongue will declare your deliverance with joy.

Lord, you will open my lips and my mouth shall show forth your praise.

For if you had desired sacrifice, I would have given it; in whole burnt offerings, you will not be pleased.

Sacrifice to God is a broken spirit; a broken and humbled heart, God will not despise.

Do good, Lord, to Zion in Your good pleasure; and let the walls of Jerusalem be built.

Then you will delight in a sacrifice of righteousness, in burnt offerings and whole burnt offerings; then calves will be offered on your altar.

Scripture Readings

It is most helpful for the development of our souls to read the Holy Scriptures on a daily basis. See the Introduction p. 13 ff. for suggestions for reading the Scriptures daily.

The Creed

It is customary to recite the Nicene Creed each day (see p. 71).

One normal place to recite the creed is immediately after the reading of the Holy Scriptures, since the creed summarizes the basic teachings of the Scriptures.

Prayers Of Thanksgivings

The following is a set of six suggested thanksgivings for each day in the week. These prayers may be used as written; they may be used in part; they may be used as suggestions for silent prayer; or they may be combined with other intercessions and thanksgivings.

Sunday

Theme: The glory of God and his love for us

Thanksgivings: Sunday Evening

Lord God, through the resurrection of Jesus Christ we see your love and eternal purposes. Help us to grow in your grace and be your people forever and ever.

Let us give thanks for:

1. The love of God that gave his only Son and for our salvation.

   Your love, O God, is deeper than ever we can imagine. To rescue a slave, you sent your Son, and in him suffered the pain of the cross. We marvel at your patience with our sins. All we can return is inadequate and imperfect. Save us -- for we cannot save ourselves -- and let your love recreate us in your image. Amen.

2. The presence of the Holy Spirit to lead us and guide us in his way.

   O Holy Spirit, you touch us at every turn. You call us to faith; you grant us a vision of Christ, and you lead us to draw closer to him. We give you thanks for guiding our steps and enlightening our minds. Keep us close to him who loved us and gave his life for us. Amen.

3. The life God has given us and our joy in praising and serving him.

   Each day is a wonder, O Lord, as we see all that you have created. We praise you for life -- for its wonder and mystery -- and for the fellowship we have with you and with those around us. We begin to see the joy of your presence as we love you and lift up those whom you call us to serve. Grant us the joy and peace of your presence. Amen.

4. The lives of all who have been channels of God's love and blessings to us.

   Lord God, we owe so much to other people; to those who having passed on before us; who preserved for us the Gospel message in the Church, leading us to you. We thank you for calling people in every generation to be your witnesses. Help us to appreciate all that you have planned for us, and help us to become -- more fully -- a faithful people, for future generations. Amen.

5. Every deed of love and kindness we have received and which we can extend.

   Father, through your Holy Spirit, you touch every human being -- for in the grace you extend to all, we experience love and kindness. We thank you, O God, for every good deed; every act of kindness we have received from others; and we praise you that we can respond in showing this same care and love in all our human relationships. Amen.

6. The sure hope and eternal promises God has for all his people.

Your word, O God, is sure; and your promises never fail. Our future is dark and meaningless, save for your grace and love. Keep us ever watchful for the coming of our Lord, who will fulfill all things, that you may be all in all, forever and ever. Amen.

Monday

Theme: Creation and providence

Thanksgivings: Monday Evening

Father, we delight in your good gifts to us, and in your holy purposes. Help us to be faithful stewards of your creation.

Let us give thanks for:

1. All of God's creation.

    We marvel, Father, as we follow your creative hand. The complexity of life; the beauty of flowers; that vastness of space all sing in harmony. We thank you, in our feeble way, for all that we have -- especially for the joys of living on your earth. Help us to trace your steps and respect every act of creation. Amen.

2. The resources of the earth.

    In your goodness to us, Almighty God, you have given us land, water, air, and space. We have a great treasure to manage, and we thank you for your generosity in all that we have received. Help us to have a proper respect for the resources of the earth, using them wisely and sharing them for the good of all your creatures. Let us be responsible stewards in your vineyard. Amen.

3. The gift of life.

   Through our joys and sorrows, our strengths and weaknesses, we choose life -- and we cling to it as the greatest of your gifts. In your love, you have shared your life with us and have touched us with your image. Make us truly grateful for such a gift and assist us that our praises and thanksgivings will be acceptable in your sight, O Lord, our strength and our Redeemer. Amen.

4. Our creative talents.

   Lord God, it is astounding to see the wonderful things human beings can do. The discoveries of the mind and their application to life; the beauty of music, art, and literature; and the creative relationships fostered between people constantly amaze us. You have given us so much. Help us to see the virtue, the truth, and the beauty you have placed into our lives -- and in so seeing, help us to be thankful. Amen.

5. Every achievement for our benefit.

   We are most fortunate people. Our lives are protected, uplifted, and made easier by the labor of others. In your love for us, you have distributed gifts to be used for the benefit of all. We thank you and praise you for every human achievement and for all the benefits we have received. May we always see your creative hand in every good gift and in every pure impulse of life. Amen.

6. God's patience with us.

   O God, we want so many things, immediately; and we often hurt other people and disregard your love and commandments. We thank you for your patience with us -- a patience we neither merit nor often respect. Help us to respond to your love, and keep our minds fixed upon your strength and your eternity. Amen.

Tuesday

Theme: Revelation and human knowledge

Thanksgivings: Tuesday Evening

Give us a genuine reverence for the truth, and such wisdom in the use of knowledge that your name will be glorified in our midst.

Let us give thanks for:

1. The revelation of God in Christ.

    Your love, O God, is deeper than we will ever comprehend. When we sinned and cut ourselves off from your presence, you came to us, lived among us, enlightened our darkness, and showed us your truth. In mercy, you have forgiven us; and in Jesus Christ, you rescued us from our sin and disobedience. Words fail us as we try to praise you and thank you. Assist us through your Spirit, that we may praise your name forever. Amen.

2. The joy of labor and our contribution to society.

    Father of all, we thank you that we can labor and produce the goods and services which help make life a joy to live. We thank you for that special feeling we have when we know that our labor and our contributions have made a difference. Help us never to flee honest work, but to see there your call to contribute to society. Let us be your instruments to bring a creative word to earth, and so claim in your name the good you would give us. Amen.

3. The joy of knowledge and our capacity to know truth.

Lord God, your word is truth and your ways are knowledge. We thank you that we have been given the gift of knowledge and are able to think your thoughts after you, even to search out your mysteries and apply that knowledge to life. Give us a thirst for truth. Keep us restless and unsatisfied until we rest our minds in your truth and bend our wills to uphold that truth. We pray that true knowledge will be our guide and enlighten all our endeavors. Amen.

4. The joy of service to other people.

We thank you, Father, that we are able to serve one another. In your wisdom you let us learn spiritual lessons as we help and teach, learn, and lean upon others. We thank you that we can share love, one with another, and in that sharing know you and your love. Help us to see your love for all people as we walk with them every day. Amen.

5. The discoveries made by human beings.

Father, there are so many good things in this world. The minds you have given us have been used in many wonderful ways.

We have learned to curb disease, repair human bodies, relieve human drudgery, and produce in abundance from the soils and minerals of the earth. We praise you for the ability to make such discoveries, and for the ability to grow and mature as human beings. Help us also to learn the harder lessons of how to share; how to care for others and how to build upon ruins, turning them into castles. Amen.

6. The freedom to build and learn.

We rejoice in the freedom you have given us, Lord. We thank you for the freedom to learn new things, to dream, and to fulfill those dreams. Help us to not abuse our freedom but to be good stewards of the talents and the opportunities we have. O Holy Spirit, stir our hearts and minds that we may have the creativity to be the people you call us to be. Amen.

Wednesday

Theme: Reconciliation and human relationships

Thanksgivings: Wednesday Evening

Help us, Father, to learn to obey as Jesus Christ our Lord obeyed; and in this obedience, let us love and serve one another -- giving and forgiving.

Let us give thanks for:

1. The obedience of Christ and his sacrifice.

    Worthy is the Lamb, O God, of infinite praise. Our feeble words can never express our gratitude for his sacrifice upon the cross. His obedience calls forth our obedience. His love, being given, calls us to respond in love. Help us in our weakness to be reconciled to one another, as our Lord Christ has reconciled us with you. Amen.

2. His bearing of the sins of the world, and his love for us.

    What wondrous love, O God, that your Son should lay aside celestial glory to come to us and save us when we were lost. Your love in Christ is ever new and always astounds us. Through your Spirit, preserve us, lest we grow cold and cease to marvel at the love which led your Son to give himself on Calvary's hill. Amen.

3. His victory over sin and death.

   Lord God, we walk with fear and guilt. We fear death. We try to hide from our sins. Then, your message of salvation conquers our gloom and calms our fears. In the resurrection of Jesus Christ from the dead, we see victory over sin and death. Your power amazes us, and your love overwhelms us. We hail your Son as Savior, and we rejoice. Amen.

4. The joy of forgiveness and a forgiving spirit.

   In our lives, keep us close to the cross, Father. Help us to remember the words of Jesus: "Forgive them, for they know not what they do." We thank you that in following Jesus Christ, we can not only learn to be forgiving, but can also experience the joy which comes from living your way. Help us to know the peace which follows honest forgiveness and true reconciliation. Free us from ourselves so that we can forgive as we have been forgiven. Amen.

5. The fruits of peace which come through forgiveness.

   Father, we have tasted your peace and the sweetness of forgiveness. From time to time, the walls which separate us crumble and the joy of love in the unity of mind and spirit shine through. Give us a forgiving spirit that your peace may abound to many, and lift us up so we can thank and praise you. Amen.

6. The opportunity to show love and service to those who need our help.

   Lord God, you sent your Son to serve and not to be served. We seek his way for our lives. We praise you that we have the opportunity to walk in service, to show your love, and to serve your people. Help us to bear one another's burdens and so fulfill the law of Christ. Open our eyes to the service we can render in his holy name. Amen.

Thursday

Theme: The Church of Jesus Christ

Thanksgivings: Thursday Evening

Grant us to be joined with Christ in this world and in the world to come, ever praising his name.

Let us give thanks for:

1. The truth of the gospel committed to the Church.

   Your word, O God, is the pearl of great price. In it we see your truth opening our eyes, directing our feet, and calling us to be your people on earth. We praise you for your word, and give thanks that its truth is available to all, challenging both the wise and the simple. Help us to follow your word, and letting go of all that hinders us, to pursue it with all our heart. Amen.

2. The promise and presence of the Holy Spirit in the Church.

   Lord Christ, you have prayed to the Father and have promised through him to send us another Counselor, the Spirit of truth. He has brought all things to mind, and has guided and delivered your Church through the centuries. We thank you for your promises kept and for the hope which burns in our hearts. Let this same Spirit dwell in us that we may walk with the same power and purpose as did the apostles in their day. Amen.

3. The divine mission of the Church and our part in it.

O Savior of the world, you sent out apostles and disciples to preach and to teach; to serve and to heal. In every age, your people have walked with a sense of divine purpose and mission. We praise you today that we too may be part of your divine work here on earth. Lift up our eyes that we may see fields ready for harvest. Lead us to claim for you the true fruit of righteousness and loving service. Amen.

4. The faithful witness of saints, martyrs, and Christians throughout the centuries.

We give you thanks, O Lord, for all your saints and martyrs who have done justly, loved mercy, and walked humbly with their God. For the great and memorable, we give you thanks. Their deeds speak of your Spirit, and their example challenges us to righteousness and holy living. For the lowly and humble, we praise you that, in their obscurity they have lifted up the name of Christ that many may know him and serve him. Amen.

5. The works of service and compassion performed in the name of Christ and his Church.

We give you thanks, O God, that even a cup of cold water given in the name of Christ will be remembered, and that the giver will not lose his reward. In your love, you call us to love people; and you give us the power to do works of loving service, ministering to the needs of others. We thank you for every good deed, and for every kind act we have received; and we pray that our gratitude may lead us more and more into your service. Amen.

6. The ministry of the word and sacrament.

We praise you, Almighty God, that in your wisdom, you have given us your word and sacraments; and we thank you for those you call to minister to us. Give us a thirst for the means of grace. Lead us to cherish your word; to thirst for your sacraments; and to call upon you in prayer. May the word made flesh be the song in our hearts. Amen.

Friday

Theme: All that meets human need

Thanksgivings: Friday Evening

Fill us with your presence -- so that in good times and in bad, in joy and in sorrow, we may overflow with peace and give witness to your eternal presence.

Let us give thanks for:

1. The cross of Christ and his priestly ministry on our behalf.

    Your cross is our only glory, O Lord Christ. Without your sacrifice, we are nothing -- lost in our sins and excluded from eternity. Through your sacrifice, death is defeated; and in your resurrection from the dead, eternity breaks in upon us. We offer our thanksgiving, O risen and living Lord, for your continuing ministry on our behalf. Unworthy as we are, we cling to your cross. Create within us a life of thanksgiving; and then mold us after your likeness. O Great High Priest, intercede for us now and in every moment. Amen.

2. The presence of Christ to strengthen and support us.

    We see you, O Lord Christ, in the bread and wine of the Eucharist. We hear you speak to us in the reading and preaching of your holy word. You touch us in prayer. You call to us in the needs of people around us. You are near to us in all of life, and we thank you for your presence. We are strong in your strength. We are courageous in your courage. We are able to love even our enemies, but only through your love. Keep us near you, now and forever. Amen.

3. The power of the Holy Spirit to lead us through every suffering and every danger.

O Holy Spirit, your presence brings joy to our hearts and comfort to our souls. We thank and praise you for leading us through every valley of deep darkness, and for giving us courage in the face of peril and danger. In our sickness, you minister to us. In times of death and sorrow, you lift us up. In good times and in bad, you lead us and give us the light of Christ. We pray that our praise will be attuned to your presence. Amen.

4. All agencies of service and every good deed done.

Lord God, we rejoice that your Spirit touches every person and that everyone can do good and show love for others. We give you thanks for people who serve the needs of others. We thank you for those who guard our safety; for those who protect our health; and for those who lift up the broken and the unfortunate. Let your Spirit fall upon all, that we may produce good works and give glory to your name. Amen.

5. Every person and organization which sets people free from pain, fear, and distress.

   In your Son, O Father, you have revealed your way -- casting out fear, relieving pain, and lifting up those in distress. We praise you that we can participate in his work and be his Body to do your will. Lead us to help every person -- every group -- which sets people free from suffering and fear. Lord, give us courage to do good -- for we are so powerless alone. Amen.

6. That we can be part of Christ's ministry in the world and serve in his name.

   O Lord Christ, you call us to be your people; to serve as your hands and feet; continuing your ministry here on earth. We thank you that we can be your instruments of healing and peace. Lord, take us, sinful as we are, and use us to speak your word and to bear your name for all to see. Teach us to serve and not be served. Amen.

Saturday

Theme: The fulfillment of God's purposes

Thanksgivings: Saturday Evening

Father, let us live by faith, walk in hope, and be renewed with your love -- until we, who call upon your name through the power of the Holy Spirit, reflect your glory and serve you forever and ever.

Let us give thanks for:

1. Those who have lived for Christ and who have brought the gospel to us.

    Lord God, we thank you for the heritage we have. We are so fortunate. In your goodness, you have given us men and women in every age who have proclaimed your gospel and who have lived saintly lives, giving us examples of faithfulness. We are a people most blessed, and we pray that we may respect our heritage by faithful obedience today, giving you the honor and glory. Amen.

2. The growth and renewal of the Church in every generation.

    Lord God, your ways amaze us. Generation after generation faithful people preach your gospel, give witness to your presence, and build your Church. You stir us from our sin and complacency. You challenge us to new and better ways. You keep your promises, and we can rest our lives in your power.

Lord God, we give you thanks and praise for your mercy and your gifts. Renew us through Jesus Christ our Lord. Amen.

3. New Christians to stand with us in the company of the saints.

We thank you, Father, for the work of your Holy Spirit through whom new souls are added to your Holy Orthodox Church. As the water of baptism seals your promise, and the food of the eucharist feeds our souls, we see your grace raising up person after person to stand with all the saints in their eternal praise of your glory. Help us today to be your witnesses and so proclaim your message to this generation. Amen.

4. Christ's promise that we shall be with him eternally.

Lord God, we praise you for your Son's promise that within your house are many rooms. Our hearts yearn for eternity and are restless until they find their rest in you. Lead us day by day that we may walk in your Spirit and be found in your eternal presence. Amen.

5. The foretaste of eternity in the Sacraments, which seal us in Christ.

Father, in your mercy you have given us signs of your love and protection. In our weakness and doubt, we receive your Sacraments and are touched with your divine grace. We give you thanks for that foretaste of your eternal presence and for the assurance that Christ is present to claim us and preserve us through all eternity. Amen.

6. The blessed hope in the Holy Spirit who applies the benefits of Christ to us.

    O Holy Spirit, power divine, your touch fills our lives with hope. We give thanks for your presence which draws us to Christ and applies to us his saving power. Open our hearts fully, that we may respond to him and reflect his presence each day. Keep before us the end of our faith, the salvation of our souls, and the eternal presence of him who loved us and gave his life for us. Amen.

On Saturdays, it is appropriate to offer prayers for those who have fallen asleep in the Lord (see: "Prayers of Commemoration," p.73).

Here one may offer other prayers, personal prayers, or silent prayer.

Concluding Prayers

John, Baptizer of Christ, remember us, so that we may be saved from our sins. For to you has been given grace to intercede for us.

Intercede for us, Holy apostles, and all you saints, so that we may be saved from danger and sorrow. We have received you as fervent defenders before the Savior.

Theotokos, beneath your compassion we seek refuge. Do not overlook our prayers, but deliver us from danger, only pure and blessed one.

My hope is the Father; my refuge, the Son; my protection, the Holy Spirit. Holy Trinity, glory to you.

Through the prayers of our holy Fathers, Lord Jesus Christ our God, have mercy on us and save us. Amen.

The Symbol of Faith

The Nicene Creed

This statement of faith was given to us by the Holy Spirit through the Holy Fathers of the Ecumenical Council held at Nicea in 325 A.D. This has served as the basic statement of the Christian religion since, and all Orthodox Christians are urged to repeat this creed, daily.

I believe in one God,
Father Almighty,
Creator of heaven and earth,
and of all things visible and invisible;

And in one Lord Jesus Christ,
the only begotten Son of God,
begotten of the Father
before all ages;

Light of Light,
true God of true God,
begotten, not created,
of one essence with the Father
Through whom all things were made.

Who for us
and for our salvation
came down from heaven
and was incarnate of the Holy Spirit
and the Virgin Mary
and became man.

He was crucified for us
Under Pontius Pilate,
And suffered and was buried;

And he rose on the third day,
according to the Scriptures,

He ascended into heaven
and is seated at the right hand of the Father;

And he will come again with glory
to judge the living and dead.
His kingdom shall have no end;

And in the Holy Spirit,
the Lord, the Creator of life,
Who proceeds from the Father,
Who together with the Father and the Son
is worshiped and glorified,
Who spoke through the prophets;

In one, holy, catholic,
and apostolic Church.

I confess one baptism
for the forgiveness of sins.

I look for the resurrection of the dead,
and the life of the age to come. Amen.

Prayers of Commemoration

The following prayers may be used to commemorate specific events in the life of Christ or in the continuing life of the Church; or Christians who have led saintly lives. These prayers are meant to point us to the full liturgical worship of the Orthodox Church. They ought to remind us that we do not pray alone, but that we join in the prayers of the whole host of God's people, now and unto the ages of ages.
Prayers which are dated may be used on that fixed date on the liturgical calendar. Prayers which do not have a date may be used for a season, such as Lent, or for several celebrations for the same person or event, such as John the Baptist.

The Life of Our Savior

Preparing For His Coming

Grant us patience, O Lord, that -- as we yearn for your presence and for your coming in power and might -- we may remain faithful to our present life and to the duties you give us each day. Amen.

The Nativity

Almighty God, for the gift of your Son we give thanks. For the light that enlightens our lives, we praise you. For the truth that has come to us through your incarnation, we give great glory. Lead us again -- through thought and in feeling -- to that lowly stable where we can see the salvation which you have brought us. Turn our thoughts from our own selves and our own strivings, and set them upon the eternity which you have prepared for us. Amen.

Epiphany (Theophany)

We thank you, Father, for your eternal plans and for your unchangeable nature. We praise you for the light of Jesus Christ, who gives us the power to become your people; and for the presence of the Holy Spirit, leading us to serve you with joy and gladness of heart. May the waters of baptism continue to flow over us, cleansing us and calling us to follow the light of Christ. Amen.

Presentation of Christ Into the Temple
February 2

Eternal God, you have called to us through prophets, priests, and saints, in seeking to make your covenant and fatherly love firm in our hearts. Help us now to say, with Simeon of old, *Lord, now lettest thou thy servant depart in peace, according to they word: for mine eyes have seen thy salvation which thou hast prepared in the presence of all peoples, a light for revelation to the Gentiles, and for glory to thy people Israel*(RSV). Amen.

The Transfiguration
August 6

As Peter, James, and John were given a glimpse into the true nature of their Lord, and as they heard the voice from the cloud saying, "This is my beloved Son," help us, O Lord, to hear your voice and to walk ever more closely the way you set before us. Amen.

Lent

Lord God, we praise you for reaching out to us and drawing us to yourself. So often, we find it hard to believe that you love us and forgive us. We know no thanksgiving to render but a contrite heart and a spirit which is given to you in humble gratitude. Help us to fast and pray that we may rejoice with our Lord when he returns to claim his own. Amen.

Palm Sunday/Holy Week

As we enter this week and recall the events in the death and resurrection of Jesus Christ, we can only bow our heads in shame for that human sin which made the cross necessary. Help us never to forget that we walk in newness of life and in righteousness -- not because of our greatness, but because of the work of Christ himself for our salvation. Amen.

Pascha (Easter)

Eternal God, we can never thank you in proper measure for the resurrection of our Lord -- knowing that in Christ, our sins are forgiven, our life is renewed, and eternity is granted to mortal flesh. Help us to give you adoration and praise, that in your presence we may find our greatest joy. Amen.

Ascension

Almighty God, as your eternal Son ascended from the earth to dwell with you in heaven -- and there lives to intercede for us -- so help us to rise above every weight of sin and so abide in him, that we may be his people and reflect his love for all to see. Amen.

Pentecost

Almighty God, who gives us the presence and power of the Holy Spirit; let his gifts so abound in us that we may be drawn closer to you and bear witness to your eternal Word, Jesus Christ, your Son, who lives and reigns with you and the Holy Spirit -- one God, forever and ever. Amen.

Honoring the *Theotokos*

The Nativity of the Theotokos
September 8

Eternal God, we are amazed when we see your hand choosing what we would never choose, and lifting up what we in our own lives we would never lift up. You chose a peasant girl to be the mother of your Son, and what we see becomes the *Theotokos* of purity and truth. Help us, pure and blessed one, to walk in faith and to rejoice in the day you were born. Amen.

The Entrance of the Theotokos Into the Temple
November 21

According to Jewish law and custom, the parents of the *Theotokos* brought her to the temple in Jerusalem. Here she was dedicated to the service of God. Help us, O Lord, to fulfill the obligations of faith -- and so grow in grace, seeking the prayers of the Mother of God, to become reflections of her eternal Son. Amen.

The Annunciation
March 25

By an angel, O Lord, you announced to the Virgin Mary her favor in your sight -- and that through her, your divine Son would take human flesh and be the Savior of the world. Help us, Almighty God, to praise and honor Mary for her purity, her faith, and her obedience, and to follow her example of trusting her Son, our Lord Jesus Christ. Amen.

The Dormition of the Theotokos
August 15

Holy Father, you chose the Virgin Mary to be the Mother of your eternal Son, our Lord Jesus Christ. Help us to rise up and call her blessed, and to hold before our eyes her example of faith, purity, and obedience. Give us the same quality of faith that led her to trust you to the very end of life. Mold our lives with your Spirit, that we may long to be pure in body and mind. Lead us to that point of obedience where we will find our true freedom in your presence. Amen.

The Forerunner

John The Baptist

Lord God, in your providence, John became your servant to preach repentance; to prepare the way for your Son; and to baptize him, fulfilling all righteousness. Help us to remember John, his message, and his obedience -- and in so remembering, lead us to repent of our sins, stand for your truth, and lift up your holy Gospel. Amen.

For Apostles and Evangelists

Mark, The Evangelist
April 25

O God, through the obedience of Mark, you have given us the Gospel message for all to read. We thank you for this witness to your love, and we pray that we may be obedient to the truth you have revealed to us. Amen.

The Apostle James
April 30

James and his brother John heard the call of Jesus and left their nets and followed him. Help us to hear the call of the Son of God, and -- leaving the allures of this world -- may we grow closer to him who loved us and gave his life for us. Amen.

The Apostle John
May 8

Lord God, let the light and truth we have received through your servant, John, dwell in our hearts and lead us to do your holy will. Help us to meditate upon the Word made flesh, as John taught and wrote -- leading us to life eternal. Amen.

The Apostle Simeon the Zealot
May 10

Simon turned his zealotry toward the Lord, and served him with strength and passion. May we, O Lord, have strengthened arms and legs to do the work of Christ, following the example of Simon each and every day. Amen.

The Apostle Bartholomew
June 11

Almighty and ever-living God, we remember today your servant Bartholomew. As you gave him grace to believe and to preach your word, so grant to us the same grace, that we may be your servants to believe and declare your presence in every circumstance. Amen.

The Apostle Jude
June 19

Humbly, Jude served the Lord and left us a warning against false teachings. Help us to follow Jude in humility and truth, seeking to grow more fully into the likeness of him who loved us and gave his life for us. Amen.

The Apostles Peter and Paul
June 29

Almighty God, your servants Peter and Paul became strong in faith through your Holy Spirit -- preaching the Word; building the Church; and, in faith, glorifying you in their martyrdom. Help us hold to their teaching and example, that your word may dwell in us, richly and that we may be united with all your people, relying upon Jesus Christ our Lord. Amen.

The Apostle Matthias
August 9

Almighty God, you chose Matthias, your faithful servant, to take the place of the unfaithful Judas and to be numbered among the Twelve. Guard now your Church, that it be served by faithful and true pastors and be delivered from every false leader. Amen.

The Apostle Thomas
October 6

Father, as you strengthened the faith of Thomas and helped him conquer his doubting, so strengthen our faith, that fears and doubts will be banished, and that we will follow the example of Thomas and preach your word near and far. Amen.

Luke, The Evangelist
October 18

Almighty God, who inspired your servant Luke the physician to set forth in the Gospel the love and healing power of your Son: Graciously continue in your Church this love and power to heal, to the praise and glory of your name. Amen.

The Apostle Philip
November 14

Almighty God, we remember the faith of your servant Philip. As he bore witness to Christ, so help us to be faithful witnesses and stand with him, glorifying your name in life and in death. Amen.

The Apostle Matthew
November 16

Father of all, your grace changes all of life. As Matthew, the despised tax collector, was touched by the love of Christ, he was transformed and became a profitable servant. Help us now to respond to the call of him who loved us and gave himself for us, Jesus Christ our Lord. Amen.

The Apostle Andrew
November 30

Almighty God, as the apostle Andrew heard your call and obeyed by bringing his brother to your Son, help us to follow his example and bring our friends and neighbors to Jesus Christ. Purify us and help us that we may speak your word and show your love. Amen.

The following prayers may be used to commemorate other Christians included on the Calendar.

Saints

Father of mercy, through Jesus Christ you make us holy and change our inward nature. We remember today (Name), one of your saints, a sheep of your flock. We remember *(here may be mentioned particular characteristics of the person)* and all those things that *he/she* did in response to your Holy Spirit. We thank you for every good deed and word of witness which has come to us because of *his/her* faithfulness. Help us to follow every good example in all your saints, that we may be gathered into fellowship with them and with your eternal Son, Jesus Christ, to the unending praise of your glory. Amen.

Martyrs

Almighty God, because of human sin your prophets and witnesses in every age have suffered even to the point of giving their lives for their faith. We remember today (Name), who gave *his/her* life for Jesus Christ, being faithful to the uttermost. Help us, as we remember *his/her* sacrifice, to so temper our living that we may be faithful in our witness and prove the power of your love and grace, through Jesus Christ our Lord. Amen.

Prophets

Father of all, your word of truth is spoken in many surprising ways. You raise up prophets and reformers to challenge us and lead us from darkness into light, helping us to see our need to change and be made new by your word. We remember today (Name), your servant, who heard your call -- obeying -- became your instrument of grace and challenge. Help us to be open to the leading of your Spirit, that we may see the new challenges you give us. Amen.

Missionaries

Almighty and everlasting God, we praise you today for the life and work of (Name), your witness and missionary to the people of (Place). We praise you for the fruit of your Spirit, which came through *his/her* faithfulness. Raise up now among us a missionary zeal that your holy Gospel may be preached in every land; and may deeds of love be practiced for all to see. Amen.

Teachers

Father, your word is truth; and all who seek truth will find your eternal word. We thank you for those teachers you have sent us to open our minds and lead us to true wisdom. We praise you today for the gift of teaching; and for the wisdom imparted by (Name), your servant. Help us to learn from *him/her,* and to be open at all times to your Spirit of truth. Let us be humble enough to be teachable, and then be wise enough to follow the truth you give us. Amen.

Bishops, Priests, Deacons, and Leaders

Almighty God, we thank you for all those who have been faithful shepherds, leading your people in worship and service. We remember today (Name), your servant, who was faithful in *his* duties, and led your Church following the one great Shepherd of the sheep, Jesus Christ our Lord. As we remember (Name), help us to follow *his* example that we may grow in grace and be joined with *him* and all your saints, forever and ever. Amen.

Prayers for the Departed

It is appropriate to offer prayers for the departed at any time, but on Saturdays we remember those who have fallen asleep before us, and we anticipate Sunday, the day of Resurrection.

Lord God, we remember *our family and friends* who have fallen asleep before us, in the hope of resurrection to life eternal. We pray that you will pardon every sin -- every transgression in word or deed -- that they and we have committed. Place them in the light of your eternal presence, where there is no more sorrow or weeping, for the former things have passed away. For you are a loving and gracious Father to whom we commit those we love. Amen.

or

Lord God, we remember the promise we have received from Jesus that *In my Father's house are many mansions, and I will come again and receive you to Myself; that where I am, there you may be also.* We pray for (Name), our *brother/sister,* that you will receive *him/her* into your eternal presence. Pardon *his/her* offenses, blotting out every sin and transgression. May the light of your presence enfold *him/her* and lift our hearts to quench every sorrow and then rekindle the hope set before us, through Jesus Christ our Lord. Amen.

Table Prayers

Prayers at mealtime not only give us an opportunity to thank God for all his provisions, but are also an appropriate way to remind ourselves that we do not live unto ourselves alone but rather to the glory of God. When we gather as a family to eat and celebrate family bonds, we give thanks to God. This is an important step in leading children to appreciate the spiritual as well as the physical side of the family table.

Prayers before a meal:

Make the sign of the cross and say,

Glory to the Father and the Son and the Holy Spirit, now and forever and to the ages of ages. Amen.

Lord have mercy.
Lord have mercy.
Lord have mercy.

Our Father, who art in heaven, hallowed be thy name. Thy kingdom come; thy will be done on earth as it is in heaven. Give us this day our daily bread, and forgive us our trespasses as we forgive those who trespass against us; and lead us not into temptation but deliver us from evil.

For Yours is the kingdom and the power and the glory, of the Father and of the Son and of the Holy Spirit, now and forever and to the ages of ages. Amen.

Then may be offered one of the following prayers:

Christ our God, bless the food and drink of your servants, for you are holy always, now and forever and to the ages of the ages. Amen.

or

Father in heaven, sustain our bodies with this food; our hearts with true friendship; and our souls with your truth. Amen.

or

Blessed are you, O Lord God, king of the universe; for you have given us food for our bodies to sustain us, you have given us food for our minds to lead us to the truth, and you have given us food for our souls, that we may draw near to you in service and praise. Amen.

or

Almighty God, send down upon us your Holy Spirit to bless this food, to sustain our lives, and to perfect the offering of ourselves to you. Amen.

or

O God, our Father, who gives food for the body and truth for the mind; make us truly grateful for the blessings of this day, that we may grow wise and strong to do your holy will. Amen.

or

Lord Jesus, be our holy guest;
Our morning joy; our evening rest.
And with our daily bread impart
Your love and peace to every heart. Amen.

After the meal, one of the following prayers may be said:

Eternal God, our Creator and Father, give us grateful hearts, for all your mercies; and make us mindful of the needs of others. Amen.

or

Blessed is God, who has mercy upon us and nourishes us from his bountiful gifts by his grace and love always, now and forever and to the ages of ages. Amen.

Abbreviations

Old Testament

Genesis	Gn
Exodus	Ex
Leviticus	Lv
Numbers	Nm
Deuteronomy	Dt
Joshua	Jos
Judges	Jdg
Ruth	Ru
1 Kingdoms (1 Samuel)	1Kg
2 Kingdoms (2 Samuel)	2Kg
3 Kingdoms (1 Kings)	3Kg
4 Kingdoms (2 Kings)	4Kg
1 Chronicles	1Ch
2 Chronicles	2Ch
1 Ezra (2 Esdras)	1Ez
2 Ezra (Ezra/2 Esdras)	2Ez
Nehemiah	Neh
Tobit	Tb
Judith	Jdt
Esther	Est
1 Maccabees	1Mc
2 Maccabees	2Mc
3 Maccabees	3Mc
Psalms	Ps
Job	Job
Proverbs of Solomon	Pr
Ecclesiastes	Ecc

Song of Solomon	SS
Wisdom of Solomon	WSol
Wisdom of Sirach	WSir
Hosea	Hos
Amos	Am
Micah	Mic
Joel	Joel
Obadiah	Ob
Jonah	Jon
Nahum	Nah
Habakkuk	Hab
Zephaniah	Zep
Haggai	Hag
Zechariah	Zec
Malachi	Mal
Isaiah	Is
Jeremiah	Jer
Baruch	Bar
Lamentations of Jeremiah	Lam
Epistle of Jeremiah	EJer
Ezekiel	Ezk
Daniel	Dan

The books with parentheses correspond to the names used in Roman or Protestant Bibles.

New Testament

Matthew	Mt
Mark	Mk
Luke	Lk
John	Jn
Acts	Acts
Romans	Rom
1 Corinthians	1Co
2 Corinthians	2Co
Galatians	Gal
Ephesians	Eph
Philippians	Php
Colossians	Col
1 Thessalonians	1Th
2 Thessalonians	2Th
1 Timothy	1Ti
2 Timothy	2Ti
Titus	Tts
Philemon	Phm
Hebrews	Heb
James	Jam
1 Peter	1Pt
2 Peter	2Pt
1 John	1Jn
2 John	2Jn
3 John	3Jn
Jude	Jude
Revelation	Rev

Daily Bible Readings -- Year I

The New Year for Orthodox worship begins with the month of September. If the Sunday Epistle and Gospel are not printed in this lectionary, please consult your parish calendar.

17th Sunday Week of the Sunday closest to August 31

Sun. Psalm 28 (29) * 33 (34)
3Kg 8:22-40

Mon. Psalm 85 (86) * 86 (87)
2Ch 6:32-7:7, Jam 2:1-13, Mk 14:53-65

Tue. Psalm 87(88) * 89(90)
3Kg 8:65-9:9, Jam 2:14-26, Mk 14:66-72

Wed. Psalm 88(89):1-18 * 88(89):19-37
3Kg 9:11-10:13, Jam 3:1-12, Mk 15:1-11

Thu. Psalm 91(92) * 90(91)
3Kg 11:1-13, Jam 3:13-4:12, Mk 15:12-21

Fri. Psalm 92(93) * 93(94):14-23
3Kg 11:26-39, Jam 4:13-5:6, Mk 15:22-32

Sat. Psalm 95(96) * 118(119):129-144
3Kg 12:1-20, Jam 5:7-12, 19-20, Mk 15:33-39

18th Sunday Week of the Sunday closest to September 7

Sun. Psalm 65(66) * 45(46)
3Kg 12:21-33

Mon.	Psalm 96(97) * 97(98) 3Kg 13:1-10, Php 1:1-11, Mk 15:40-47
Tue.	Psalm 98(99), 99(100) * 100(101) 3Kg 16:23-34, Php 1:12-30, Mk 16:1-20
Wed.	Psalm 101(102):1-11 * 101(102):12-28 3Kg 17:1-24, Php 2:1-11, Mt 2:1-12
Thu.	Psalm 102(103) * 104(105):1-15 3Kg 18:1-19, Php 2:12-30, Mt 2:13-23
Fri.	Psalm 103(104):1-23 * 103(104):24-35 3Kg 18:20-40, Php 3:1-16, Mt 3:1-12
Sat.	Psalm 105(106):1-8, 43-48 * 118(119):145-160 3Kg 18:41-19:8, Php 3:17-4:7, Mt 3:13-17

19th Sunday Week of the Sunday closest to September 14

Sun.	Psalm 92(93) * 62(63) 3Kg 19:8-21
Mon.	Psalm 106(107):1-16 * 106(107):17-32 3Kg 21:1-16, 1Co 1:1-19, Mt 4:1-11
Tue.	Psalm 106(107):33-43 * 109(110), 110(111) 3Kg 21:17-29, 1Co 1:20-31, Mt 4:12-17
Wed.	Psalm 111(112) * 112(113) 3Kg 22:1-28, 1Co 2:1-13, Mt 4:18-25
Thu.	Psalm 113(114) * 114(115) 3Kg 22:29-45, 1Co 2:14-3:15, Mt 5:1-10

Fri.	Psalm 117(118):1-18 * 117(118):19-29 4Kg 1:2-17, 1Co 3:16-23, Mt 5:11-16
Sat.	Psalm 115(116), 116(117) * 118(119):161-176 4Kg 2:1-18, 1Co 4:1-7, Mt 5:17-20

20th Sunday Week of the Sunday closest to September 21

Sun.	Psalm 95(96) * 66(67) 4Kg 4:8-37
Mon.	Psalm 120(121) * 121(122), 122(123) 4Kg 5:1-19, 1Co 4:8-21, Mt 5:21-26
Tue.	Psalm 123(124), 124(125) * 125(126), 126(127) 4Kg 5:19-27, 1Co 5:1-8, Mt 5:27-37
Wed.	Psalm 127(128), 128(129) * 129(130), 130(131) 4Kg 6:1-23, 1Co 5:9-6:8, Mt 5:38-48
Thu.	Psalm 131(132) * 132(133), 133(134) 4Kg 9:1-16, 1Co 6:12-20, Mt 6:1-6,16-18
Fri.	Psalm 134(135):1-7,15-21 * 135(136) 4Kg 9:17-37, 1Co 7:1-9, Mt 6:7-15
Sat.	Psalm 136(137):1-6 * 137(138) 4Kg 11:1-20a, 1Co 7:10-24, Mt 6:19-24

21st Sunday Week of the Sunday closest to September 28

Sun.	Psalm 117(118):19-29 * 97(98) 4Kg 17:1-18
Mon.	Psalm 138(139) * 139(140) 4Kg 17:24-41, 1Co 7:25-31, Mt 6:25-34

Tue.	Psalm 140(141) * 141(142)
	2Ch 29:1-3, 30:1-27, 1Co 7:32-40, Mt 7:1-12
Wed.	Psalm 142(143) * 143(144)
	4Kg 18:9-25, 1Co 8:1-13, Mt 7:13-21
Thu.	Psalm 144(145):1-7 * 144(145):8-21
	4Kg 18:28-37, 1Co 9:1-15, Mt 7:22-29
Fri.	Psalm 145(146) * 146(147)
	4Kg 19:1-20, 1Co 9:16-27, Mt 8:1-17
Sat.	Psalm 148 * 149:1-5, 150
	4Kg 19:21-36, 1Co 10:1-13, Mt 8:18-27

22nd Sunday Week of the Sunday closest to October 5

Sun.	Psalm 145(146) * 102(103)
	4Kg 20:1-21
Mon.	Psalm 1, 2:1-8 * 3, 4
	4Kg 21:1-18, 1Co 10:14-11:1, Mt 8:28-34
Tue.	Psalm 5:1-8, 11-12 * 6:1-9
	4Kg 22:1-13, 1Co 11:2, 17-22, Mt 9:1-8
Wed.	Psalm 7:1-11, 16(17) * 8
	4Kg 22:14-23:3, 1Co 11:23-34, Mt 9:9-17
Thu.	Psalm 9:1-10 * 9:21 ff. (10:1-12, 16-18)
	4Kg 23:4-25, 1Co 12:1-11, Mt 9:18-26
Fri.	Psalm 10(11) * 11(12)
	4Kg 23:36-24:17, 1Co 12:12-26, Mt 9:27-34
Sat.	Psalm 12(13), 14(15) * 118(119):1-16
	Jer 42(35):1-19, 1Co 12:27-13:3, Mt 9:35-10:4

23rd Sunday Week of the Sunday closest to October 12

Sun.   Psalm 146(147:1-11) * 110(111)
          Jer 43(36):1-10

Mon.   Psalm 13(14), 15(16) * 16(17)
          Jer 43(36):11-26, 1Co 13:1-13, Mt 10:5-15

Tue.   Psalm 17(18):1-16 * 17(18):17-31
          Jer 43(36):27-44(37):2, 1Co 14:1-12
          Mt 10:16-23

Wed.   Psalm 18(19) * 19(20)
          Jer 44(37):3-21, 1Co 14:13-25, Mt 10:24-33

Thu.   Psalm 20(21):1-7 * 22(23)
          Jer 45(38):1-13, 1Co 14:26-40, Mt 10:34-42

Fri.   Psalm 21(22):1-21 * 21(22):22-31
          Jer 45(38):14-28, 1Co 15:1-11, Mt 11:1-6

Sat.   Psalm 23(24) * 118(119):17-32
          4Kg 25:8-12, 22-26, 1Co 15:12-29, Mt 11:7-15

24th Sunday Week of the Sunday closest to October 19

Sun.   Psalm 148 * 111(112)
          Jer 46(39):11-18)

Mon.   Psalm 24(25) * 25(26)
          Jer 36(29):1,4-14, 1Co 15:30-41, Mt 11:16-24

Tue.   Psalm 26(27) * 27(28)
          Jer 47(40):7-41:3, 1Co 15:41-50, Mt 11:25-30

Wed.   Psalm 28(29) * 29(30)
          Jer 48(41):4-18, 1Co 15:51-58, Mt 12:1-14

Thu.	Psalm 30(31):1-8 * 30(31):9-24 Jer 49(42), 1Co 16:1-9, Mt 12:15-21
Fri.	Psalm 31(32) * 32(33) Jer 50(43):1-13, 1Co 16:10-24, Mt 12:22-32
Sat.	Psalm 34(35):9-18 * 118(119):33-48 Jer 51(44):1-14, Phm 1-25, Mt 12:33-42

25th Sunday Week of the Sunday closest to October 26

Sun.	Psalm 149 * 114(115) Jer 52(44):21-28
Mon.	Psalm 33(34):1-10 * 33(34):12-23 Jer 51:31-35 (45:1-5), Rev 1:4-20, Mt 12:43-50
Tue.	Psalm 35(36) * 36(37):1-11 Lam 1:1-9, Rev 4:1-11, Mt 13:1-9
Wed.	Psalm 36(37):12-29 * 36(37):30-40 Lam 2:8-15, Rev 5:1-10, Mt 13:10-17
Thu.	Psalm 37(38):1-9 * 37(38):10-22 Lam 2:16-22, Rev 5:11-6:11, Mt 13:18-23
Fri.	Psalm 38(39) * 39(40) Lam 4:1-22, Rev 6:12-7:4, Mt 13:24-30
Sat.	Psalm 40(41) * 118(119):49-64 Lam 5:1-22, Rev 7:4-17, Mt 13:31-35

26th Sunday Week of the Sunday closest to November 2

Sun.	Psalm 150 * 144(145) 1Ez 1:1-11

Mon.	Psalm 41(42) * 42(43) 1Ez 3:1-13, Rev 10:1-11, Mt 13:36-43
Tue.	Psalm 43 (44):1-8 * 44(45) 1Ez 4:33-48, Rev 11:1-19, Mt 13:44-52
Wed.	Psalm 45(46) * 46(47) Hag 1:1-2:9, Rev 12:1-12, Mt 13:53-58
Thu.	Psalm 47(48) * 48(49) Zec 1:7-17, Rev 14:1-13, Mt 14:1-12
Fri.	Psalm 49(50):1-15 * 50(51) 1Ez 5:1-17, Rev 15:1-8, Mt 14:13-21
Sat.	Psalm 51(52) * 118(119):65-80 1Ez 6:1-22, Rev 17:1-14, Mt 14:22-36

27th Sunday Week of the Sunday closest to November 9

Sun.	Psalm 23(24) * 18(19) 2Ez 1:1-11
Mon.	Psalm 52(53) * 53(54) 2Ez 2:1-20, Rev 18:1-8, Mt 15:1-20
Tue.	Psalm 54(55):1-8 * 55(56) 2Ez 4:1-23, Rev 18:9-20, Mt 15:21-28
Wed.	Psalm 56(57) * 60(61) 2Ez 5:1-19, Rev 18:21-24, Mt 15:29-39
Thu.	Psalm 61(62) * 62(63):1-8 1Mc 1:1-28, Rev 19:1-10, Mt 16:1-12

Fri.	Psalm 63(64) * 64(65) 1Mc 1:41-63, Rev 19:11-26, Mt 16:13-20
Sat.	Psalm 65(66) * 118(119):81-96 1Mc 2:1-28, Rev 20:1-6, Mt 16:21-28

28th Sunday **Week of the Sunday closest to November 16**

Sun.	Psalm 28(29) * 33(34) 1Mc 2:29-43
Mon.	Psalm 66(67) * 69(70) 1Mc 2:49-70, Rev 20:7-15, Mt 17:1-13
Tue.	Psalm 67(68):1-18 * 67(68):21-36 1Mc 3:1-24, Rev 21:1-8, Mt 17:14-21
Wed.	Psalm 68(69):1-13a * 68(69):13b-21,29-36 1Mc 3:25-41, Rev 21:9-21, Mt 17:22-27
Thu.	Psalm 70(71):1-14 * 70(71):15-24 1Mc 3:42-60, Rev 21:22-22:5, Mt 18:1-9
Fri.	Psalm 72(73):1-14 * 72(73):15-28 1Mc 4:1-25, Rev 22:6-13, Mt 18:10-20
Sat.	Psalm 71(72) * 118(119):97-112 1Mc 4:36-59, Rev 22:14-21, Mt 18:21-35

29th Sunday **Week of the Sunday closest to November 23**

Sun.	Psalm 117(118) * 144(145) Is 19:19-25
Mon.	Psalm 73(74):1-12 * 73(74):13-23 Joel 3:1-5, 1Pt 1:1-12, Mt 19:1-12

Tue.	Psalm 74(75) * 75(76) Nah 1:1-13, 1Pt 1:13-25, Mt 19:13-22
Wed.	Psalm 76(77) * 77(78):1-7 Ob 15-21, 1Pt 2:1-10, Mt 19:23-30
Thu.	Psalm 79(80) * 80(81) Zep 3:1-13, 1Pt 2:11-25, Mt 20:1-16
Fri.	Psalm 81(82) * 83(84) Is 24:1, 4-23, 1Pt 3:13-4:6, Mt 20:17-28
Sat.	Psalm 84(85) * 118(119):113-128 Mic 7:11-20, 1Pt 4:7-19, Mt 20:29-34

30th Sunday *Week of the Sunday closest to November 30*

Sun.	Psalm 23(24) * 18(19) Is 1:1-9
Mon.	Psalm 85(86) * 86(87) Is 1:10-20, 1Th 1:1-10, Lk 20:1-8
Tue.	Psalm 87(88) * 89(90) Is 1:21-31, 1Th 2:1-12, Lk 20:9-18
Wed.	Psalm 88(89):1-18 * 88(89):19-37 Is 2:1-11, 1Th 2:13-20, Lk 20:19-26
Thu.	Psalm 91(92) * 90(91) Is 2:12-21, 1Th 3:1-13, Lk 20:27-40
Fri.	Psalm 92(93) * 93(94):14-23 Is 3:8-15, 1Th 4:1-12, Lk 20:41-21:4

Sat.	Psalm 95(96) * 118(119):129-144 Is 4:2-6, 1Th 4:13-18, Lk 21:5-19

31st Sunday Week of the Sunday closest to December 6

Sun.	Psalm 28(29) * 33(34) Is 5:1-7
Mon.	Psalm 96(97) * 97(98) Is 5:8-12, 18-23, 1Th 5:1-11, Lk 21:20-28
Tue.	Psalm 98(99), 99(100) * 100(101) Is 5:13-17, 24-25, 1Th 5:12-28, Lk 21:29-38
Wed.	Psalm 101(102):1-11 * 101(102):12-29 Is 6:1-13, 2Th 1:1-12, Jn 7:53-8:11
Thu.	Psalm 102(103) * 104(105):1-15 Is 7:1-9, 2Th 2:1-12, Lk 22:1-13
Fri.	Psalm 103(104):1-23 * 103(104):24-35 Is 7:10-25, 2Th 2:13-3:5, Lk 22:14-30
Sat.	Psalm 105(106):1-8,43-48 * 118(119):145-160 Is 8:1-15, 2Th 3:6-18, Lk 22:31-38

32nd Sunday Week of the Sunday closest to December 13

Sun.	Psalm 65(66) * 45(46) Is 13:6-13
Mon.	Psalm 106(107):1-16 * 106(107):17-32 Is 8:16-9:1, 2Pt 1:1-11, Lk 22:39-53
Tue.	Psalm 106(107):33-43 * 109(110),110(111) Is 9:1-7, 2Pt 1:12-21, Lk 22:54-69

Wed.	Psalm 111(112) * 112(113) Is 9:8-17, 2Pt 2:1-10a, Mk 1:1-18
Thu.	Psalm 113(114) * 114(115) Is 9:18-10:4, 2Pt 2:10b-16, Mt 3:1-12
Fri.	Psalm 117(118):1-18 * 117(118):19-29 Is 10:5-19, 2Pt 2:17-22, Mt 11:2-15
Sat.	Psalm 115(116),116(117) * 118(119):161-176 Is 10:20-27, Jude 17-25, Lk 3:1-9

Sunday Before Christmas
Begin these readings on the day indicated.

Dec.	
18	Psalm 120(121) * 121(122) Is 11:1-9, Eph 6:10-20, Jn 3:16-21
19	Psalm 122(123) * 123(124) Is 11:10-16, Rev 20:1:10, Jn 5:30-47
20	Psalm 124(125) * 125(126), 126(127) Is 28:9-22, Rev 20:11-21:8, Lk 1:5-25
21	Psalm 127(128), 128(129) * 129(130), 130(131) Is 29:13-24, Rev 21:9-21, Lk 1:26-38
22	Psalm 131(132) * 132(133), 133(134) Is 32:1-9, Rev 21:22-22:5, Lk 1:39-56
23	Psalm 134(135):1-7,15-21 * 135(136) Is 33:1-10, Rev 22:6-11, Lk 1:57-66
24	Psalm 136(137):1-6 * 137(138) Is 35:1-10, Rev 22:12-17, 21, Lk 1:67-80

Christmas and Week After

25	Psalm 99(100) * 94(95) Zec 2:10-13, 1Jn 4:7-16, Jn 3:31-36
26	Psalm 138(139) * 139(140) 2Ch 24:17-22, Acts 6:1-7, Mt 1:18-25
27	Psalm 140(141) * 141(142) Pr 8:22-30, 1Jn 5:1-12, Jn 13:20-35
28	Psalm 142(143) * 143(144) Is 49:13-23, Php 3:1-11, Mt 18:1-14
29	Psalm 144(145):1-7 * 144(145):8-21 Is 12:1-6, Rev 1:1-8, Jn 7:37-52
30	Psalm 145(146) * 146(147) Is 25:1-9, Rev 1:9-20, Jn 7:53-8:11
31	Psalm 148 * 149:1-5, 150 Is 26:1-6, 2Co 5:16-6:2, Jn 8:12-19

The Second Week After Christmas

Continue reading by date until the First Sunday after the Epiphany.

Jan.

1	Psalm 102(103) * 89(90) Gn 17:12a,15-16, Col 2:6-12, Jn 16:23b-30
2	Psalm 33(34) * 32(33) Gn 12:1-7, Heb 11:1-12, Jn 6:35-42, 48-50
3	Psalm 67(68) * 71(72) Gn 28:10-22, Heb 11:13-22, Jn 10:7-17

4   Psalm 84(85) * 86(87)
           Ex 3:1-5, Heb 11:23-31, Jn 14:6-14

5   Psalm 2 * 97(98)
           Jos. 1:1-9, Heb 11:32-12:2, Jn 15:1-16

6   Epiphany — Psalm 148 * 149:1-5, 150
           Is 52: 7-10, Rev 21:22-27, Mt 12:14-21

Additional Days After Epiphany

The Psalms and Readings for the dated days after the Epiphany are used only until the First Sunday after Epiphany.

Jan.
7   Psalm 102(103) * 103(104)
           Is 52:3-6, Rev 2:1-7, Jn 2:1-11

8   Psalm 116(117), 117(118) * 111(112), 112(113)
           Is 59:15-21, Rev 2:8-17, Jn 4:46-54

9   Psalm 120(121), 121(122), 122(123) * 130(131), 131(132),
           Is 63:1-5, Rev 2:18-29, Jn 5:1-15

10   Psalm 137(138), 138(139):1-17 * 146(147)
           Is 65:1-9, Rev 3:1-6, Jn 6:1-14

11   Psalm 148. 150 * 90(91), 91(92)
           Is 65:13-16, Rev 3:7-13, Jn 6:15-27

12   Psalm 97(98), 98(99) * 103(104)
           Is 66:1-2,22-23, Rev 3:14-22, Jn 9:1-12,35-38

Week of First Sunday After Epiphany
Sunday between January 7 & 13

Sun.	Psalm 23(24) * 18(19) Is 40:1-11
Mon.	Psalm 1, 2:1-8 * 3, 4 Is 40:12-23, Eph 1:1-14, Mk 1:1-13
Tue.	Psalm 5:1-8, 11-12 * 6:1-9 Is 40:25-31, Eph. 1:15-23, Mk 1:14-28
Wed.	Psalm 7:1-11,17 * 8 Is 41:1-16, Eph 2:1-10, Mk 1:29-45
Thu.	Psalm 9:1-10 * 9:22-39(10:1-12,16-18) Is 41:17-29, Eph 2:11-22, Mk 2:1-12
Fri.	Psalm 10(11) * 11(12) Is 42:1-17, Eph 3:1-13, Mk 2:13-22
Sat.	Psalm 12(13), 14(15) * 118(119):1-16 Is 43:1-13, Eph 3:14-21, Mk 2:23-3:6

Use the following weekly readings until the Sunday of the Publican and the Pharisee which starts the Triodion leading to Great Lent. Consult your parish calendar for the beginning of the Triodion.

Week of the Second Sunday After Epiphany
Sunday between January 14 & 20

Sun.	Psalm 28(29) * 33(34) Is 43:14-44:5

Mon.	Psalm 13(14), 15(16) * 16(17) Is 44:6-8, 21-23, Eph 4:1-16, Mk 3:7-19a
Tue.	Psalm 17(18):1-16 * 17(18):17-31 Is 44:9-20, Eph 4:17-32, Mk 3:19b-35
Wed.	Psalm 18(19) * 19(20) Is 44:24-45:7, Eph 5:1-14, Mk 4:1-20
Thu.	Psalm 20(21) * 22(23) Is 45:5-17, Eph 5:15-33, Mk 4:21-34
Fri.	Psalm 21(22):1-21 * 21(22):22-31 Is 45:18-25, Eph 6:1-9, Mk 4:35-41
Sat.	Psalm 23(24) * 118(119):17-32 Is 46:1-13, Eph 6:10-24, Mk 5:1-20

Week of the Third Sunday After Epiphany
Sunday between January 21 & 27

Sun.	Psalm 65(66) * 45(46) Is 47:1-15
Mon.	Psalm 24(25) * 25(26) Is 48:1-11, Gal 1:1-17, Mk 5:25-34
Tue.	Psalm 26(27) * 27(28) Is 48:12-21, Gal 1:18-2:10, Mk 6:1-13
Wed.	Psalm 28(29) * 29(30) Is 49:1-12, Gal 2:11-21, Mk 6:14-29
Thu.	Psalm 30(31):1-8 * 30(31):9-24 Is 49:13-23, Gal 3:1-14, Mk 6:30-46

Fri.	Psalm 31(32) * 32(33) Is 50:1-11, Gal. 3:15-22, Mk 6:47-56
Sat.	Psalm 34(35):9-18 * 118(119):33-48 Is 51:1-8, Gal 3:23-29, Mk 7:1-23

Week of the Fourth Sunday After Epiphany
Sunday between January 28 & February 3

Sun.	Psalm 92(93) * 62(63) Is 51:9-16
Mon.	Psalm 33(34):1-10 * 33(34):11-22 Is 51:17-23, Gal 4:1-11, Mk 7:24-37
Tue.	Psalm 35(36) * 36(37):1-11 Is 52:1-12, Gal 4:12-20, Mk 8:1-10
Wed.	Psalm 36(37):12-29 * 36(37):30-40 Is 54:1-17, Gal 4:21-31, Mk 8:11-26
Thu.	Psalm 37(38):1-9 * 37(38):10-22 Is 55:1-13, Gal 5:1-15, Mk 8:27-9:1
Fri.	Psalm 38(39) * 39(40) Is 56:1-8, Gal. 5:16-24, Mk 9:2-13
Sat.	Psalm 40(41) * 118(119):49-64 Is 57:3-13, Gal 5:25-6:10, Mk 9:14-29

Week of the Fifth Sunday After Epiphany
Sunday between February 4 & 10

Sun.	Psalm 95(96) * 66(67) Is 57:14-21

Mon.	Psalm 41(42) * 42(43) Is 58:1-12, Gal 6:11-18, Mk 9:30-41
Tue.	Psalm 43(44):1-8 * 44(45) Is 59:1-15a, 2Ti 1:1-14, Mk 9:42-50
Wed.	Psalm 45(46) * 46(47) Is 59:15b-21, 2Ti 1:15-2:13, Mk 10:1-16
Thu.	Psalm 47(48) * 48(49) Is 60:1-17, 2Ti 2:14-26, Mk 10:17-31
Fri.	Psalm 49(50):1-15 * 50(51) Is 61:1-9, 2Ti 3:1-17, Mk 10:32-45
Sat.	Psalm 51(52) * 118(119):65-80 Is 61:10-62:5, 2Ti 4:1-8, Mk 10:46-52

If more weeks are needed, turn to the week after the Week of All Saints.

Sunday of the Publican and the Pharisee
This is the beginning of the Triodion leading to Great Lent. Consult your parish calendar for this date.

Sun.	Psalm 117(118):18-29 * 97(98) Is 62:6-12 2, Tim 3:10-15, Lk 18:10-14
Mon.	Psalm 52(53) * 53(54) Is 63:1-6, 1Ti 1:1-17, Mk 11:1-11
Tue.	Psalm 54(55):1-8 * 55(56) Is 63:7-14, 1Ti 1:18-2:8, Mk 11:12-26
Wed.	Psalm 56(57) * 60(61) Is 63:15-64:9, 1Ti 3:1-16, Mk 11:27-12:12

Thu.	Psalm 61(62) * 62(63):1-8 Is 65:1-12, 1Ti 4:1-16, Mk 12:13-27
Fri.	Psalm 63(64) * 64(65) Is 65:17-25, 1Ti 5:17-25, Mk 12:28-34
Sat	Psalm 65(66) * 118(119):81-96 Is 66:1-6, 1Ti 6:6-21, Mk 12:35-44

Sunday of the Prodigal Son

Sun.	Psalm 145(146) * 102(103) Is 66:7-14, 1Co 6:12-20, Lk 15:11-32
Mon.	Psalm 66(67) * 69(70) Ru 1:1-14, 2Co 1:1-11, Mt 5:1-12
Tue.	Psalm 67(68):1-18 * 67(68):24-35 Ru 1:15-22, 2Co 1:12-22, Mt 5:13-20
Wed.	Psalm 68(69):1-13a * 68(69):13b-21, 29-36 Ru 2:1-13, 2Co 1:23-2:17, Mt 5:21-26
Thu.	Psalm 70(71):1-14 * 70(71):15-24 Ru 2:14-23, 2Co 3:1-18, Mt 5:27-37
Fri.	Psalm 72(73):1-14 * 72(73):15-28 Ru 3:1-18, 2Co 4:1-12, Mt 5:38-48
Sat.	Psalm 71(72) * 118(119):97-112 Ru 4:1-17, 2Co 4:13-5:10, Mt 6:1-6

Judgment Sunday (Meat-Fare Sunday)

Sun.	Psalm 146(147:1-11) * 110(111) Dt 4:1-8, 1Co 8:8-9:2, Mt 25:31-46

Mon. Psalm 73(74):1-12 * 73(74):13-23
Dt 4:9-14, 2Co 10:1-18, Mt 6:7-15

Tue. Psalm 74(75) * 75(76)
Dt 4:15-24, 2Co 11:1-21a, Mt 6:16-23

Wed. Psalm 76(77) * 77(78):1-7
Dt 4:25-31, 2Co 11:21b-33, Mt 6:24-34

Thu. Psalm 79(80) * 80(81)
Dt 4:32-40, 2Co 12:1-10, Mt 7:1-12

Fri. Psalm 81(82) * 83(84)
Dt 5:1-22, 2Co 12:11-21, Mt 7:13-21

Sat. Psalm 84(85) * 118(119):113-128
Dt 5:22-33, 2Co 13:1-14, Mt 7:22-29

Forgiveness Sunday (Cheese-Fare Sunday)

Sun. Psalm 147(148) * 111(112)
Dt 6:1-9, Rom 13:11-14:4, Mt 6:14-21

Mon. Psalm 1, 2:1-8 * 3, 4
Jonah 3:1-4:11, Heb 12:1-14, Lk 18:9-14

Tue. Psalm 5:1-8,11-12 * 6:1-9
Dt 6:16-25, Heb 2:1-10, Jn 1:19-28

Wed. Psalm 7:1-11, 17 * 8
Dt 6:10-15, Heb 2:11-18, Jn 1:1-18

Thu. Psalm 9:1-10 * 9:22-39(10):1-12,16-18
Dt 7:7-11, Tts 1:1-16, Jn 1:29-34

Fri.	Psalm 10(11) * 11(12) Dt 7:12-16, Tts 2:1-15, Jn 1:35-42
Sat.	Psalm 12(13), 14(15) * 118(119):1-16 Dt 7:17-26, Tts 3:1-15, Mt 6:1-13

The First Week of Lent/The Sunday of Orthodoxy

Sun.	Psalm 23(24) * 18(19) Dt 8:1-10, Heb 11:24-26,32-40, Jn 1:43-51
Mon.	Psalm 13(14), 15(16) * 16(17) Dt 8:11-20, Heb 2:11-18, Jn 2:1-12
Tue.	Psalm 17(18):1-16 * 17(18):17-31 Dt 9:4-12, Heb 3:1-11, Jn 2:13-22
Wed.	Psalm 18(19) * 19(20) Dt 9:13-21, Heb 3:12-19, Jn 2:23-3:15
Thu.	Psalm 20(21):1-7 * 22(23) Dt 9:23-10:5, Heb 4:1-10, Jn 3:16-21
Fri.	Psalm 21(22):1-21 * 21(22):22-31 Dt 10:12-22, Heb 4:11-16, Jn 3:22-36
Sat.	Psalm 23(24) * 118(119):17-32 Dt 11:18-28, Heb 5:1-10, Jn 4:1-26

The Second Week of Lent

Sun.	Psalm 28(29) * 33(34) Jer 1:1-10, Heb 1:10-2:3, Mk 2:1-12
Mon.	Psalm 24(25) * 25(26) Jer 1:11-19, Rom 1:1-15, Jn 4:27-42

Tue.	Psalm 26(27) * 27(28) Jer 2:1-13, Rom 1:16-25, Jn 4:43-54
Wed.	Psalm 28(29) * 29(30) Jer 3:6-18, Rom 1:28-2:11, Jn 5:1-18
Thu.	Psalm 30(31):1-8 * 30(31):9-24 Jer 4:9-10,19-28, Rom 2:12-24, Jn 5:19-29
Fri.	Psalm 31(32) * 32(33) Jer 5:1-9, Rom 2:25-3:18, Jn 5:30-47
Sat.	Psalm 34(35):9-18 * 118(119):33-48 Jer 5:20-31, Rom 3:19-31, Jn 7:1-13

The Third Week of Lent

Sun.	Psalm 65(66) * 45(46) Jer 6:9-15, Heb 4:14-5:6, Mk 8:34-9:1
Mon.	Psalm 33(34):1-11 * 33(34):11-23 Jer 7:1-15, Rom 4:1-12, Jn 7:14-36
Tue.	Psalm 35(36) * 36(37):1-11 Jer 7:21-33, Rom 4:13-25, Jn 7:37-52
Wed.	Psalm 36(37):12-29 * 36(37):30-40 Jer 8:18-9:6, Rom 5:1-11, Jn 8:12-20
Thu.	Psalm 37(38):1-9 * 37(38):10-22 Jer 10:11-21, Rom 5:12-21, Jn 8:21-32
Fri.	Psalm 38(39) * 39(40) Jer 11:1-8,14-20, Rom 6:1-11, Jn 8:33-47
Sat.	Psalm 40(41) * 118(119):49-64 Jer 13:1-11, Rom 6:12-23, Jn 8:47-59

The Fourth Week of Lent

Sun.	Psalm 92(93) * 62(63) Jer 14:1-9,17-22, Heb 6:13-20, Mk 9:17-31
Mon.	Psalm 41(42) * 42(43) Jer 16:10-21, Rom 7:1-12, Jn 6:1-15
Tue.	Psalm 43(44):1-8 * 44(45) Jer 17:15-23, Rom 7:13-25, Jn 6:16-27
Wed.	Psalm 45(46) * 46(47) Jer 18:1-11, Rom 8:1-11, Jn 6:27-40
Thu.	Psalm 47(48) * 48(49) Jer 22:13-23, Rom 8:12-27, Jn 6:41-51
Fri.	Psalm 49(50):1-15 * 50(51) Jer 23:1-8, Rom 8:28-39, Jn 6:52-59
Sat.	Psalm 51(52) * 118(119):65-80 Jer 23:9-15, Rom 9:1-18, Jn 6:60-71

The Fifth Week of Lent

Sun.	Psalm 95(96) * 66(67) Jer 23:16-32, Heb 9:11-14, Mk 10:32-45
Mon.	Psalm 52(53) * 53(54) Jer 24:1-10, Rom 9:19-33, Jn 9:1-17
Tue.	Psalm 54(55):1-8 * 55(56) Jer 25:8-17, Rom 10:1-13, Jn 9:18-41
Wed.	Psalm 56(57) * 60(61) Jer 32:17-25(25:30-38) Rom 10:14-21, Jn 10:1-18

Thu.	Psalm 61(62) * 62(63):1-8 Jer 33(26):1-16, Rom 11:1-12, Jn 10:19-42
Fri.	Psalm 63(64) * 64(65) Jer 36(29):1, 4-13, Rom 11:13-24, Jn 11:1-27
Sat.	Psalm 65(66) * 118(119):81-96 Jer 38(31):27-34, Rom 11:25-36, Jn 11:28-44

Week of Palm Sunday

Palm Sun.	Psalm 28(29) * 102(103) Zec 9:9-12, Php 4:4--9, Jn 12:1-18
Holy Mon.	Psalm 26(27) * 6 Jer 12:1-16, Php 3:1-14, Jn 12:9-19
Holy Tue.	Psalm 30(31) * 31(32) Jer 15:10-21, Php 3:15-21, Jn 12:20-26
Holy Wed.	Psalm 54(55) * 142(143) Jer 17:5-10, 14-17, Php 4:1-13, Jn 12:27-36
Holy Thu.	Psalm 55(56) * 63(64) Jer 20:7-11, 1Co 10:14-17; 11:27-32 Jn 17:1-26
Holy Fri.	Psalm 21(22) * 68(69) Gn 22:1-14, 1Pt 1:10-20, Jn 19:38-42
Holy Sat.	Psalm 29(30) * 22(23) Job 19:21-27a, Heb 4:1-16, Rom 8:1-11

Great and Holy Pascha

Easter	Psalm 148, 149, 150 * 117(118)
Day	Rom 6:3-11, Mt 28:1-20 *morning*
	Acts 1:1-8, Jn 1:1-17 *evening*
Mon.	Psalm 66(67) * 69(70)
	Jon 2:1-9, Acts 2:14, 22-32, Jn 14:1-14
Tue.	Psalm 67(68):1-18 * 67(68):24-35
	Is 30:18-21, Acts 2:36-47, Jn 14:15-31
Wed.	Psalm 68(69):1-13a * 68(69):13b-21,29-36
	Mic 7:7-15, Acts 3:1-10, Jn 15:1-11
Thu.	Psalm 70(71):1-14 * 70(71):15-24
	Ezk 37:1-14, Acts 3:11-26, Jn 15:12-27
Fri.	Psalm 72(73):1-14 * 72(73):15-28
	Dan 12:1-4,13, Acts 4:1-12, Jn 16:1-15
Sat.	Psalm 71(72) * 118(119):97-112
	Is 25:1-9, Acts 4:13-31, Jn 16:16-33

Sunday of Saint Thomas

Sun.	Psalm 117(118):19-29 * 97(98)
	Is 43:8-13, Acts 5:12-20, Jn 20:19-31
Mon.	Psalm 73(74):1-12 * 73(74):13-23
	Dan 1:1-21, 1 Jn 1:1-10, Jn 17:1-11
Tue.	Psalm 74(75) * 75(76)
	Dan 2:1-16, 1 Jn 2:1-11, Jn 17:12-19
Wed.	Psalm 76(77) * 77(78):1-7
	Dan 2:17-30, 1 Jn 2:12-17, Jn 17:20-26

Thu.	Psalm 79(80) * 80(81) Dan 2:31-49, 1 Jn 2:18-29, Lk 3:1-14
Fri.	Psalm 81(82) * 83(84) Dan 3:1-18, 1 Jn 3:1-10, Lk 3:15-22
Sat.	Psalm 84(85) * 118(119):113-128 Dan 3:19-30, 1 Jn 3:11-18, Lk 4:1-13

Sunday of the Myrrh-Bearers

Sun.	Psalm 145(146) * 102(103) Dan 4:1-18, Acts 6:1-7, Mk 15:43-16:8
Mon.	Psalm 85 (86) * 86 (87) Dan 4:19-27, 1Jn 3:19-4:6, Lk 4:14-30
Tue.	Psalm 87(88) * 89(90) Dan 4:28-37, 1Jn 4:7-21, Lk 4:31-37
Wed.	Psalm 88(89):1-18 * 88(89):19-37 Dan 5:1-12, 1Jn 5:1-12, Lk 4:38-44
Thu.	Psalm 91(92) * 90(91) Dan 5:13-30, 1Jn 5:13-21, Lk 5:1-11
Fri.	Psalm 92(93) * 93(94):14-23 Dan 6:1-15, 2Jn 1-13, Lk 5:12-26
Sat.	Psalm 95(96) * 118(119):129-144 Dan 6:16-28, 3Jn 1-15, Lk 5:27-39

Sunday of the Paralytic

Sun.	Psalm 146(147:1-11) * 110(111) WSol 1:1-15, Acts 9:32-42, Jn 5:1-15

Mon.	Psalm 96(97) * 97(98) WSol 1:16-2:11, 21-24, Col 1:1-14, Lk 6:1-11
Tue.	Psalm 98(99), 99(100) * 100(101) WSol 3:1-9, Col 1:15-23, Lk 6:12-26
Wed.	Psalm 101(102):1-11 * 101(102):12-28 WSol 4:16-5:8, Col 1:24-2:7, Lk 6:27-38
Thu.	Psalm 102(103) * 104(105):1-15 WSol 5:9-23, Col 2:8-23, Lk 6:39-49
Fri.	Psalm 103(104):1-23 * 103(104):24-35 WSol 6:12-23, Col 3:1-11, Lk 7:1-17
Sat.	Psalm 105(106):1-8,43-48 * 118(119):145-160 WSol 7:1-14, Col 3:12-17, Lk 7:18-35

Sunday of the Samaritan Woman

Sun.	Psalm 147(148) * 111(112) WSol 7:22-8:1, Acts 11:19-26, 29-30, Jn 4:4-42
Mon.	Psalm 106(107):1-16 * 106(107):17-32 WSol 9:1, 7-18, Col 3:18-4:18, Lk 7:36-50
Tue.	Psalm 106(107):33-43 * 109(110), 110(111) WSol 10:1-21, Rom 12:1-21, Lk 8:1-15
Wed.	Psalm 111(112) * 112(113) WSol 13:1-9, Rom 13:1-14, Lk 8:16-25
Thu.	Psalm 113(114) * 116:1-9 WSol 14:27-15:3, Rom 14:1-12, Lk 8:26-39

Fri.	Psalm 117(118):1-18 * 117(118):19-29 WSol 16:15-17:1, Rom 14:13-23, Lk 8:40-56
Sat.	Psalm 115(116:10-19), 116(117) * 118(119):161-176 WSol 19:1-8, 18-22, Rom 15:1-13, Lk 9:1-17

Sunday of the Blind Man

Sun.	Psalm 149 * 114(115) WSir 43:1-12, 27-32, Acts 16:16-34 John 9:1-38
Mon.	Psalm 120(121) * 121(122), 122(123) Dt 18:9-14, Jam 1:1-15, Lk 9:18-27
Tue.	Psalm 123(124), 124(125) * 125(126), 126(127) Dt 18:15-22, Jam 1:16-27, Lk 11:1-13
Wed.	Psalm 127(128), 128(129) * 129(130), 130(131) Bar 3:24-37, Jam 5:13-18, Lk 12:22-31
Thu.	Psalm 8 * 95(96) Ezk 1:1-14, 24-28b, Heb 2:5-18, Mt 28:16-20
Fri.	Psalm 134(135):1-7, 15-21 * 135(136) Ezk 1:28-3:3, Heb 4:14-5:6, Lk 9:28-36
Sat.	Psalm 136(137):1-6 * 137(138) Ezk 3:4-17, Heb 5:7-14, Lk 9:37-50

Sunday of the Holy Fathers

Sun.	Psalm 150 * 144(145) Ezk 3:16-27, Acts 20:16-18, 28-36, Jn 17:1-13

Mon.	Psalm 138(139) * 139(140) Ezk 4:1-17, Heb 6:1-12, Lk 9:51-62
Tue.	Psalm 140(141) * 141(142) Ezk 7:10-15, 23b-27, Heb 6:13-20, Lk 10:1-17
Wed.	Psalm 142(143) * 143(144) Ezk 11:14-25, Heb 7:1-17, Lk 10:17-24
Thu.	Psalm 144(145):1-7 * 144(145):8-21 Ezk 18:1-4, 19-32, Heb 7:18-28, Lk 10:25-37
Fri.	Psalm 145(146) * 146(147) Ezk 34:17-31, Heb 8:1-13, Lk 10:38-42
Sat.	Psalm 148 * 149:1-5,150 Ezk 43:1-12, Heb 9:1-14, Lk 11:14-23

Pentecost

Pentecost	Psalm 117(118) * 144(145) Is 11:1-9, Acts 2:1-11, Jn 7:37-52; 8:12
Mon.	Psalm 52(53) * 53(54) Is 63:7-14, 2Ti 1:1-14, Lk 11:24-36
Tue.	Psalm 54(55):1-8 * 55(56) Is 63:15-64:9, 2Ti 1:15-2:13, Lk 11:37-52
Wed.	Psalm 56(57) * 60(61) Is 65:1-12, 2Ti 2:14-26, Lk 11:53-12:12
Thu.	Psalm 61(62) * 62(63):1-8 Is 65:17-25, 2Ti 3:1-17, Lk 12:13-31

Fri.	Psalm 63(64) * 64(65) Is 66:1-6, 2Ti 4:1-8, Lk 12:32-48
Sat.	Psalm 65(66) * 118(119):81-96 Is 66:7-14, 2Ti 4:9-22, Lk 12:49-59
Sun.	**Sunday of All Saints** Psalm 111 * 112 WSol 3:1-9, Heb. 11:33-12:2 Mt 10:32-33, 37-38
Mon.	Psalm 66(67) * 69(70) Ru 1:1-18, 1Ti 1:1-17, Lk 13:1-9
Tue.	Psalm 67(68):1-18 * 67(68):24-35 Ru 1:19-2:13, 1Ti 1:18-2:8, Lk 13:10-17
Wed.	Psalm 68(69):1-13a * 68(69):13b-21, 29-36 Ru 2:14-23, 1Ti 3:1-16, Lk 13:18-30
Thu.	Psalm 70(71):1-14 * 70(71):15-24 Ru 3:1-18, 1Ti 4:1-16, Lk 13:31-35
Fri.	Psalm 72(73):1-14 * 72(73):15-28 Ru 4:1-17, 1Ti 5:17-25, Lk 14:1-11
Sat.	Psalm 71(72) * 118(119):97-112 Dt 1:1-8, 1Ti 6:6-21, Lk 14:12-24

After finishing the week of All Saints look down in the next few weekly readings until you find the one corresponding to the next Sunday on the calendar.

3rd Sunday   **Week of the Sunday closest to May 25**

Sun.	Psalm 146(147:1-11) * 110(111) Dt 4:1-9

Mon.	Psalm 73(74):1-12 * 73(74):13-23 Dt 4:9-14, 2Co 1:1-11, Lk 14:25-35
Tue.	Psalm 74(75) * 75(76) Dt 4:15-24, 2Co 1:12-22, Lk 15:1-10
Wed.	Psalm 76(77) * 77(78):1-7 Dt 4:25-31, 2Co 1:23-2:17, Lk 15:1-2, 11-32
Thu.	Psalm 79(80) * 80(81) Dt 4:32-40, 2Co 3:1-18, Lk 16:1-9
Fri.	Psalm 81(82) * 83(84) Dt 5:1-22, 2Co 4:1-12, Lk 16:10-18
Sat.	Psalm 84(85) * 118(119):113-128 Dt 5:22-33, 2Co 4:13-5:10, Lk 16:19-31

4th Sunday — *Week of the Sunday closest to June 1*

Sun.	Psalm 23(24) * 18(19) Dt 11:1-12
Mon.	Psalm 85 (86) * 86 (87) Dt 11:13-19, 2Co 5:11-6:2, Lk 17:1-10
Tue.	Psalm 87(88) * 89(90) Dt 12:1-12, 2Co 6:3-7:1, Lk 17:11-19
Wed.	Psalm 88(89):1-18 * 88(89):19-37 Dt 13:1-11, 2Co 7:2-16, Lk 17:20-37
Thu.	Psalm 91(92) * 89(91) Dt 16:18-20, 17:14-20, 2Co 8:1-16, Lk 18:1-8

Fri.	Psalm 92(93) * 93(94):14-23 Dt 26:1-11, 2Co 8:16-24, Lk 18:9-14
Sat.	Psalm 95(96) * 118(119):129-144 Dt 29:2-15, 2Co 9:1-15, Lk 18:15-30

5th Sunday — *Week of the Sunday closest to June 8*

Sun.	Psalm 28(29) * 33(34) Dt 29:16-29
Mon.	Psalm 96(97) * 97(98) Dt 30:1-10, 2Co 10:1-18, Lk 18:31-43
Tue.	Psalm 98(99), 99(100) * 100(101) Dt 30:11-20, 2Co 11:1-21a, Lk 19:1-10
Wed.	Psalm 101(102):1-11 * 101(102):12-28 Dt 31:30-32:14, 2Co 11:21b-33, Lk 19:11-27
Thu.	Psalm 102(103) * 104(105):1-15 WSir 44:19-45:5, 2Co 12:1-10, Lk 19:28-40
Fri.	Psalm 103(104):1-23 * 103(104):24-35 WSir 45:6-16, 2Co 12:11-21, Lk 19:41-48
Sat.	Psalm 105(106):1-8, 43-48 * 118(119):145-160 WSir 46:1-10, 2Co 13:1-14, Lk 20:1-8

6th Sunday — *Week of the Sunday closest to June 15*

Sun.	Psalm 65(66) * 45(46) WSir 46:11-20
Mon.	Psalm 106(107):1-16 * 106(107):17-32 1Kg 1:1-20, Acts 1:1-14, Lk 20:9-19

Tue.	Psalm 106(107):33-43 * 109(110), 110(111) 1Kg 1:21-2:11, Acts 1:15-26, Lk 20:19-26
Wed.	Psalm 111(112) * 112(113) 1Kg 2:12-26, Acts 2:1-21, Lk 20:27-40
Thu.	Psalm 113(114) * 116:1-9 1Kg 2:27-36, Acts 2:22-36, Lk 20:41-21:4
Fri.	Psalm 117(118):1-18 * 117(118):19-29 1Kg 3:1-21, Acts 2:37-47, Lk 21:5-19
Sat.	Psalm 115(116), 116(117) * 118(119):161-176 1Kg 4:1b-11, Acts 4:32-5:11, Lk 21:20-28

7th Sunday   *Week of the Sunday closest to June 22*

Sun.	Psalm 92(93) * 62(63) 1Kg 4:12-22
Mon.	Psalm 120(121) * 121(122), 122(123) 1Kg 5:1-12, Acts 5:12-26, Lk 21:29-36
Tue.	Psalm 123(124), 124(125) * 125(126), 126(127) 1Kg 6:1-16, Acts 5:27-42, Lk 21:37-22:13
Wed.	Psalm 127(128), 128(129) * 129(130), 130(131) 1Kg 7:2-17, Acts 6:1-15a, Lk 22:14-23
Thu.	Psalm 131(132) * 132(133), 133(134) 1Kg 8:1-22, Acts 6:15-7:16, Lk 22:24-30
Fri.	Psalm 134(135):1-7,15-21 * 135(136) 1Kg 9:1-14, Acts 7:17-29, Lk 22:31-38

Sat.	Psalm 136(137):1-6 * 127(128) 1Kg 9:15-10:1, Acts 7:30-43, Lk 22:39-51
8th Sunday	**Week of the Sunday closest to June 29**
Sun.	Psalm 92(93) * 62(63) 1Kg 10:1-16
Mon.	Psalm 138(139) * 139(140) 1Kg 10:17-27, Acts 7:44-8:1a, Lk 22:52-62
Tue.	Psalm 140(141) * 141(142) 1Kg 11:1-15, Acts 8:1-13, Lk 22:63-71
Wed.	Psalm 142(143) * 143(144) 1Kg 12:1-6,16-25, Acts 8:14-25, Lk 23:1-12
Thu.	Psalm 144(145):1-7 * 144(145):8-21 1Kg 13:5-18, Acts 8:26-40, Lk 23:13-25
Fri.	Psalm 145(146) * 146(147) 1Kg 13:19-14:15, Acts 9:1-9, Lk 23:26-31
Sat.	Psalm 147(148) * 148(149):1-5, 150 1Kg 14:16-30, Acts 9:10-19a, Lk 23:32-43
9th Sunday	**Week of the Sunday closest to July 6**
Sun.	Psalm 95(96) * 66(67) 1Kg 14:36-45
Mon.	Psalm 1, 2:1-8 * 3, 4 1Kg 15:1-3, 7-23, Acts 9:19b-31, Lk 23:44-56a
Tue.	Psalm 5:1-8, 11-12 * 6:1-9 1Kg 15:24-35, Acts 9:32-43, Lk 23:56b-24:11

Wed.	Psalm 7:1-11, 17 * 8
	1Kg 16:1-13, Acts 10:1-16, Lk 24:12-35
Thu.	Psalm 9:1-10 * 9:21-39 (10):1-12, 16-18
	1Kg 16:14-23, Acts 10:17-33, Lk 24:36-53
Fri.	Psalm 10(11) * 11(12)
	1Kg 17:1-11, Acts 10:34-48, Mk 1:1-13
Sat.	Psalm 12(13), 14(15) * 118(119):1-16
	1Kg 17:12-30, Acts 11:1-18, Mk 1:14-28

10th Sunday — Week of the Sunday closest to July 13

Sun.	Psalm 117(118):19-29 * 97(98)
	1Kg 18-1-9
Mon.	Psalm 13(14), 15(16) * 16(17)
	1Kg 18:10-19, Acts 11:19-30, Mk 1:29-45
Tue.	Psalm 17(18):1-16 * 17(18):17-31
	1Kg 19:1-18, Acts 12:1-17, Mk 2:1-12
Wed.	Psalm 18(19) * 19(20)
	1Kg 20:1-23, Acts 12:18-25, Mk 2:13-22
Thu.	Psalm 20(21):1-7 * 22(23)
	1Kg 20:24-42, Acts 13:1-12, Mk 2:23-3:6
Fri.	Psalm 21(22):1-21 * 21(22):22-31
	1Kg 21:1-15, Acts 13:13-25, Mk 3:7-19a
Sat.	Psalm 23(24) * 118(119):17-32
	1Kg 22:1-23, Acts 13:26-43, Mk 3:19a-35

11th Sunday	**Week of the Sunday closest to July 20**
Sun.	Psalm 145(146) * 102(103) 1Kg 23:7-18
Mon.	Psalm 24(25) * 25(26) 1Kg 24:1-22, Acts 13:44-52, Mk 4:1-20
Tue.	Psalm 26(27) * 27(28) 1Kg 25:1-22, Acts 14:1-18, Mk 4:21-34
Wed.	Psalm 28(29) * 29(30) 1Kg 25:23-44, Acts 14:19-28, Mk 4:35-41
Thu.	Psalm 30(31):1-8 * 30(31):9-25 1Kg 28:3-20, Acts 15:1-11, Mk 5:1-20
Fri.	Psalm 31(32) * 32(33) 1Kg 31:1-13, Acts 15:12-21, Mk 5:21-43
Sat.	Psalm 34(35):9-18 * 118(119):33-48 2Kg 1:1-16, Acts 15:22-35, Mk 6:1-13
12th Sunday	**Week of the Sunday closest to July 27**
Sun.	Psalm 147 * 110(111) 2Kg 1:17-27
Mon.	Psalm 33(34):1-10 * 33(34):11-22 2Kg 2:1-11, Acts 15:36-16:5, Mk 6:14-29
Tue.	Psalm 35(36) * 36(37):1-11 2Kg 3:6-21, Acts 16:6-15, Mk 6:30-46
Wed.	Psalm 36(37):12-29 * 36(37):30-40 2Kg 3:22-39, Acts 16:16-24, Mk 6:47-56

Thu.	Psalm 37(38):1-9 * 37(38):10-22 2Kg 4:1-12, Acts 16:25-40, Mk 7:1-23
Fri.	Psalm 38(39) * 39(40) 2Kg 5:1-12, Acts 17:1-15, Mk 7:24-37
Sat.	Psalm 40(41) * 118(119):49-64 2Kg 5:22-6:11, Acts 17:16-34, Mk 8:1-10

13th Sunday Week of the Sunday closest to August 3

Sun.	Psalm 147(148) * 111(112) 2Kg 6:12-23
Mon.	Psalm 41(42) * 42(43) 2Kg 7:1-17, Acts 18:1-11, Mk 8:11-21
Tue.	Psalm 43(44):1-8 * 44(45) 2Kg 7:18-29, Acts 18:12-28, Mk 8:22-33
Wed.	Psalm 45(46) * 46(47) 2Kg 9:1-13, Acts 19:1-10, Mk 8:34-9:1
Thu.	Psalm 47(48) * 48(49) 2Kg 11:1-27, Acts 19:11-20, Mk 9:2-13
Fri.	Psalm 49(50):1-15 * 50(51) 2Kg 12:1-14, Acts 19:21-41, Mk 9:14-29
Sat.	Psalm 51(52) * 118(119):65-80 2Kg 12:15-31, Acts 20:1-16, Mk 9:30-41

14th Sunday Week of the Sunday closest to August 10

Sun.	Psalm 149 * 114(115) 2Kg 13:1-22

Mon.	Psalm 52(53) * 53(54) 2Kg 13:23-39, Acts 20:17-38, Mk 9:42-50
Tue.	Psalm 54(55):1-8 * 55(56) 2Kg 14:1-20, Acts 21:1-14, Mk 10:1-16
Wed.	Psalm 56(57) * 60(61) 2Kg 14:21-33, Acts 21:15-26, Mk 10:17-31
Thu.	Psalm 61(62) * 62(63):1-8 2Kg 15:1-18, Acts 21:27-36, Mk 10:32-45
Fri.	Psalm 63(64) * 64(65) 2Kg 15:19-37, Acts 21:37-22:16, Mk 10:46-52
Sat.	Psalm 65(66) * 118(119):81-96 2Kg 16:1-23, Acts 22:17-29, Mk 11:1-11

15th Sunday   *Week of the Sunday closest to August 17*

Sun.	Psalm 150 * 144(145) 2Kg 17:1-23
Mon.	Psalm 66(67) * 69(70) 2Kg 17:24-18:8, Acts 22:30-23:11 Mk 11:12-26
Tue.	Psalm 67(68):1-18 * 67(68):24-35 2Kg 18:9-18, Acts 23:12-24, Mk 11:27-12:12
Wed.	Psalm 68(69):1-13a * 68(69):13b-21,29-36 2Kg 18:19-33, Acts 23:23-35, Mk 12:13-27
Thu.	Psalm 70(71):1-14 * 70(71):15-24 2Kg 19:1-24, Acts 24:1-23, Mk 12:28-34

Fri.	Psalm 72(73):1-14 * 72(73):15-28 2Kg 19:25-43, Acts 24:24-25:12, Mk 12:35-44
Sat.	Psalm 71(72) * 118(119):97-112 2Kg 23:1-7, 13-17, Acts 25:13-27, Mk 13:1-13

16th Sunday   Week of the Sunday closest to August 24

Sun.	Psalm 23(24) * 18(19) 2Kg 24:1-2, 10-25
Mon.	Psalm 73(74):1-12 * 73(74):13-23 3Kg 1:5-31, Acts 26:1-23, Mk 13:14-27
Tue.	Psalm 74(75) * 75(76) 3Kg 1:38-2:4, Acts 26:24-27:8, Mk 13:28-37
Wed.	Psalm 76(77) * 77(78):1-7 3Kg 3:1-15, Acts 27:9-26, Mk 14:1-11
Thu.	Psalm 79(80) * 80(81) 3Kg 3:15-27, Acts 27:27-44, Mk 14:12-26
Fri.	Psalm 81(82) * 83(84) 3Kg 5:5-10-6:1-7, Acts 28:1-16, Mk 14:27-42
Sat.	Psalm 84(85) * 118(119):113-128 3Kg 8:20-41, Acts 28:17-31, Mk 14:43-52

Daily Bible Readings ~ Year II

The New Year for Orthodox worship begins with the month of September

17th Sunday   **Week of the Sunday closest to August 31**

Sun.   Psalm 28(29) * 33(34)
Job 11:1-9, 13-20

Mon.   Psalm 85(86) * 86(87)
Job 12:1-6, 13-25, Acts 11:19-30, Jn 8:21-32

Tue.   Psalm 87(88) * 89(90)
Job 12:1; 13:3-17, 21-27, Acts 12:1-17
Jn 8:33-47

Wed.   Psalm 88(89):1-18 * 88(89):19-37
Job 12:1; 14:1-22, Acts 12:18-25, Jn 8:47-59

Thu.   Psalm 91(92) * 90(91)
Job 16:16-22; 17:1, 13-16, Acts 13:1-12
Jn 9:1-17

Fri.   Psalm 92(93) * 93(94):14-23
Job 19:1-7, 14-27, Acts 13:13-25, Jn 9:18-41

Sat.   Psalm 95(96) * 118(119):129-144
Job 22:1-4, 21-23:7, Acts 13:26-43, Jn 10:1-18

18th Sunday   **Week of the Sunday closest to September 7**

Sun.   Psalm 65(66) * 45(46)
Job 25:1-6; 27:1-6

Mon.	Psalm 96(97) * 97(98) Job 27:1-23, Acts 13:44-52, Jn 10:19-30
Tue.	Psalm 98(99), 99(100) * 100(101) Job 29:1-20, Acts 14:1-18, Jn 10:31-42
Wed.	Psalm 101(102):1-11 * 101(102):12-28 Job 29:1; 30:1-2, 16-31, Acts 14:19-28 Jn 11:1-16
Thu.	Psalm 102(103) * 104(105):1-15 Job 29:1; 31:1-23, Acts 15:1-11, Jn 11:17-29
Fri.	Psalm 103(104):1-23 * 103(104):24-35 Job 29:1; 31:24-40, Acts 15:12-21, Jn 11:30-44
Sat.	Psalm 105(106):1-8, 43-48 * 118(119):145-160 Job 38:1-17, Acts 15:22-35, Jn 11:45-54

19th Sunday Week of the Sunday closest to September 14

Sun.	Psalm 92(93) * 62(63) Job 38:1, 18-41
Mon.	Psalm 106(107):1-16 * 106(107):17-32 Job 40:1-24, Acts 15:36-16:5, Jn 11:55-12:8
Tue.	Psalm 106(107):33-43 * 109(110), 110(111) Job 40:1; 41:1-11, Acts 16:6-15, Jn 12:9-19
Wed.	Psalm 111(112) * 112(113) Job 42:1-17, Acts 16:16-24, Jn 12:20-26
Thu.	Psalm 113(114) * 114(115) Job 28:1-28, Acts 16:25-40, Jn 12:27-36a

Fri.	Psalm 117(118):1-18 * 117(118):19-29 Est 1:1-19, Acts 17:1-15, Jn 12:36b-43
Sat.	Psalm 115(116), 116(117) * 118(119):161-176 Est 2:5-8, 15-23, Acts 17:16-34, Jn 12:44-50

20th Sunday   Week of the Sunday closest to September 21

Sun.	Psalm 95(96) * 66(67) Est 3:1-13
Mon.	Psalm 120(121) * 121(122), 122(123) Est 4:4-17, Acts 18:1-11, Lk 1:1-4; 3:1-14
Tue.	Psalm 123(124), 124(125) * 125(126), 126(127) Est 5:1-14, Acts 18:12-28, Lk 3:15-22
Wed.	Psalm 127(128), 128(129) * 129(130), 130(131) Est 6:1-14, Acts 19:1-10, Lk 4:1-13
Thu.	Psalm 131(132) * 132(133), 133(134) Est 7:1-10, Acts 19:11-20, Lk 4:14-30
Fri.	Psalm 134(135):1-7,15-21 * 135(136) Est 8:1-8,15-17, Acts 19:21-41, Lk 4:31-37
Sat.	Psalm 136(137):1-6 * 137(138) Est 9:1-32, Acts 20:1-16, Lk 4:38-44

21st Sunday   Week of the Sunday closest to September 28

Sun.	Psalm 117(118):19-29 * 97(98) Hos 1:1-2:1
Mon.	Psalm 138(139) * 139(140) Hos 2:2-15, Acts 20:17-38, Lk 5:1-11

Tue.	Psalm 140(141) * 141(142) Hos 2:16-23, Acts 21:1-14, Lk 5:12-26
Wed.	Psalm 142(143) * 143(144) Hos 3:1-5, Acts 21:15-26, Lk 5:27-39
Thu.	Psalm 144(145):1-7 * 144(145):8-21 Hos 4:1-10, Acts 21:27-36, Lk 6:1-11
Fri.	Psalm 145(146) * 146(147) Hos 4:11-19, Acts 21:37-22:16, Lk 6:12-26
Sat.	Psalm 148 * 149:1-5, 150 Hos 5:1-7, Acts 22:17-29, Lk 6:27-38
22nd Sunday	**Week of the Sunday closest to October 5**
Sun.	Psalm 145(146) * 102(103) Hos 5:8-6:6
Mon.	Psalm 1, 2:1-8 * 3, 4 Hos 6:7-7:7, Acts 22:30-23:11, Lk 6:39-49
Tue.	Psalm 5 * 6 Hos 7:8-16, Acts 23:12-24, Lk 7:1-17
Wed.	Psalm 7:1-11 * 8 Hos 8:1-14, Acts 23:23-35, Lk 7:18-35
Thu.	Psalm 9:1-10 * 9:21ff (10:1-12, 16-18) Hos 9:1-9, Acts 24:1-23, Lk 7:36-50
Fri.	Psalm 10(11) * 11(12) Hos 9:10-17, Acts 24:24-25:12, Lk 8:1-15

| Sat. | Psalm 12(13), 14(15) * 118(119):1-16 |
| | Hos 10:1-15, Acts 25:13-27, Lk 8:16-25 |

23rd Sunday   Week of the Sunday closest to October 12

| Sun. | Psalm 146(147:1-11) * 110(111) |
| | Hos 11:1-11 |

| Mon. | Psalm 13(14), 15(16) * 16(17) |
| | Hos 12:1-7, Acts 26:1-23, Lk 8:26-39 |

| Tue. | Psalm 17(18):1-16 * 17(18):17-31 |
| | Hos 12:7-15, Acts 26:24-27:8, Lk 8:40-56 |

| Wed. | Psalm 18(19) * 19(20) |
| | Hos 13:1-3, Acts 27:9-26, Lk 9:1-17 |

| Thu. | Psalm 20(21):1-7 * 22(23) |
| | Hos 13:4-8, Acts 27:27-44, Lk 9:18-27 |

| Fri. | Psalm 21(22):1-21 * 21(22):22-32 |
| | Hos 13:9-15, Acts 28:1-16, Lk 9:28-36 |

| Sat. | Psalm 23(24) * 118(119):17-32 |
| | Hos 14:1-9, Acts 28:17-31, Lk 9:37-50 |

24th Sunday   Week of the Sunday closest to October 19

| Sun. | Psalm 147(148) * 111(112) |
| | WSir 4:1-10 |

| Mon. | Psalm 24(25) * 25(26) |
| | WSir 4:20-5:7, Rev 7:1-8, Lk 9:51-62 |

| Tue. | Psalm 26(27) * 27(28) |
| | WSir 6:5-17, Rev 7:9-17, Lk 10:1-16 |

Wed.	Psalm 28(29) * 29(30) WSir 7:4-14, Rev 8:1-13, Lk 10:17-24
Thu.	Psalm 30(31)1:1-8 * 30(31):9-25 WSir 10:1-18, Rev 9:1-12, Lk 10:25-37
Fri.	Psalms 31(32) * 32(33) WSir 11:2-20, Rev 9:13-21, Lk 10:38-42
Sat.	Psalm 34(35):9-18 * 118(119):33-48 WSir 15:9-20, Rev 10:1-11, Lk 11:1-13

25th Sunday   Week of the Sunday closest to October 26

Sun.	Psalm 149 * 114(116): 1-9 WSir 18:19-32
Mon.	Psalm 33(34):1-11 * 33(34):12-23 WSir 19:4-17, Rev 11:1-14, Lk 11:14-26
Tue.	Psalm 35(36) * 36(37):1-11 WSir 24:1-12, Rev 11:14-19, Lk 11:27-36
Wed.	Psalm 36(37):12-29 * 36(37):30-40 WSir 28:14-26, Rev 12:1-6, Lk 11:37-52
Thu.	Psalm 37(38):1-9 * 37(38):10-23 WSir 31:12-18, 25-32:2, Rev 12:7-17 Lk 11:53-12:12
Fri.	Psalm 38(39) * 39(40) WSir 34:1-8, 18-22, Rev 13:1-10, Lk 12:13-31
Sat.	Psalm 40(41) * 118(119):49-64 WSir 35:1-17, Rev 13:11-18, Lk 12:32-48

26th *Sunday* **Week of the Sunday closest to November 2**

Sun. Psalm 150 * 144(145)
WSir 36:1-17

Mon. Psalm 41(42) * 42(43)
WSir 38:24-34, Rev 14:1-13, Lk 12:49-59

Tue. Psalm 43 (44):1-9 * 44(45)
WSir 43:1-22, Rev 14:14-15:8, Lk 13:1-9

Wed. Psalm 45(46) * 46(47)
WSir 43:23-33, Rev 16:1-11, Lk 13:10-17

Thu. Psalm 47(48) * 48(49)
WSir 44:1-15, Rev 16:12-21, Lk 13:18-30

Fri. Psalm 49(50):1-15 * 49(50):16-23
WSir 50:1, 11-24, Rev 17:1-18, Lk 13:31-35

Sat. Psalm 51(52) * 118(119):65-80
Zep 3:14-20, Rev. 18:1-14, Lk 14:1-11

27th *Sunday* **Week of the Sunday closest to November 9**

Sun. Psalm 23(24) * 18(19)
WSir 51:13-22

Mon. Psalm 52(53) * 53(54)
Joel 1:15-2:2, Rev 18:15-24, Lk 14:12-24

Tue. Psalm 54(55):1-8 * 55(56)
Joel 2:3-11, Rev 19:1-10, Lk 14:25-35

Wed. Psalm 56(57) 60(61)
Joel 2:12-19, Rev 19:11-21, Lk 15:1-10

Thu.	Psalm 61(62) * 62(63):1-8 Joel 2:21-27, Jam 1:1-15, Lk 15:1-2,11-32
Fri.	Psalm 63(64) * 64(65) Joel 3:1-5, Jam 1:16-27, Lk 16:1-9
Sat.	Psalm 65(66) * 118(119):81-96 Joel 4:1-17, Jam 2:1-13, Lk 16:10-18

28th Sunday   Week of the Sunday closest to November 16

Sun.	Psalm 28(29) * 33(34) Hab 1:1-2:1
Mon.	Psalm 66(67) * 69(70) Hab 2:1-4,9-20, Jam 2:14-26, Lk 16:19-31
Tue.	Psalm 67(68):1-18 * 67(68):24-36 Hab 3:1-19, Jam 3:1-12, Lk 17:1-10
Wed.	Psalm 68(69):1-13a * 68(69):13b-21, 29-36 Mal 1:1-14, Jam 3:13-4:12, Lk 17:11-19
Thu.	Psalm 70(71):1-14 * 70(71):15-24 Mal 2:1-16, Jam 4:13-5:6, Lk 17:20-37
Fri.	Psalm 72(73):1-14 * 72(73):15-28 Mal 3:1-12, Jam 5:7-12, Lk 18:1-8
Sat.	Psalm 71(72) * 118(119):97-112 Mal 3:13-23, Jam 5:13-20, Lk 18:9-14

29th Sunday   Week of the Sunday closest to November 23

Sun.	Psalm 117(118) * 144(145) Zec 9:9-16

Mon.	Psalm 73(74):1-12 * 73(74):13-23 Zec 10:1-12, Gal. 6:1-10, Lk 18:15-30
Tue.	Psalm 74(75) * 75(76) Zec 11:4-17, 1Co 3:10-23, Lk 18:31-43
Wed.	Psalm 76(77) * 77(78):1-7 Zec 12:1-10, Eph 1:3-14, Lk 19:1-10
Thu.	Psalm 79(80) * 80(81) Zec 13:1-9, Eph 1:15-23, Lk 19:11-27
Fri.	Psalm 81(82) * 83(84) Zec 14:1-11, Rom 15:7-13, Lk 19:28-40
Sat.	Psalm 84(85) * 118(119):113-128 Zec 14:12-21, Php 2:1-11, Lk 19:41-48

30th Sunday Week of the Sunday closest to November 30

Sun.	Psalm 23(24) * 18 (19) Am 1:1-5,13-2:8
Mon.	Psalm 85(86) * 86(87) Am 2:6-16, 2Pt 1:1-11, Mt 21:1-11
Tue.	Psalm 87(88) * 89(90) Am 3:1-11, 2Pt 1:12-21, Mt 21:12-22
Wed.	Psalm 88(89):1-18 * 88(89):19-37 Am 3:12-4:5, 2Pt 3:1-10, Mt 21:23-32
Thu.	Psalm 91(92) * 90(91) Am 4:6-13, 2Pt 3:10-18, Mt 21:33-46

Fri.	Psalm 92(93) * 93(94):14-23 Am 5:1-17, Jude 1-16, Mt 22:1-14
Sat.	Psalm 95(96) * 118(119):129-144 Am 5:18-27, Jude 17-25, Mt 22:15-22

31st Sunday   Week of the Sunday closest to December 6

Sun.	Psalm 28(29) * 33(34) Am 6:1-14
Mon.	Psalm 96(97) * 97(98) Am 7:1-9, Rev 1:1-8, Mt 22:23-33
Tue.	Psalm 98(99),99(100) * 100(101) Am 7:10-17, Rev 1:9-16, Mt 22:34-46
Wed.	Psalm 101(102):1-11 * 101(102):12-28 Am 8:1-14, Rev 1:17-2:7, Mt 23:1-12
Thu.	Psalm 102(103) * 104(105):1-15 Am 9:1-10, Rev 2:8-17, Mt 23:13-26
Fri.	Psalm 103(104):1-23 * 103(104):24-35 Hag 1, Rev 2:18-29, Mt 23:27-39
Sat.	Psalm 104(105) * 105(106):1-8, 43-48 * 118(119):145-160 Hag 2:1-9, Rev 3:1-6, Mt 24:1-14

32nd Sunday Week of the Sunday closest to December 13

Sun.	Psalm 65(66) * 45(46) Am 9:11-15
Mon.	Psalm 106(107):1-16 * 106(107):17-32 Zec 1:7-17, Rev 3:7-13, Mt 24:15-31

Tue.	Psalm 106(107):33-43 * 109(110), 110(111) Zec 2:1-13, Rev 3:14-22, Mt 24:32-44
Wed.	Psalm 111(112) * 112(113) Zec 3:1-10, Rev 4:1-8, Mt 24:45-51
Thu.	Psalm 113(114) * 114(115) Zec 4:1-14, Rev 4:9-5:5, Mt 25:1-13
Fri.	Psalm 117(118):1-18 * 117(118):19-29 Zec 7:8-8:8, Rev 5:6-14, Mt 25:14-30
Sat.	Psalm 115(116),116(117) * 118(119):161-176 Zec 8:9-17, Rev 6:1-17, Mt 25:31-46

Sunday Before Christmas

Begin these readings on the day indicated.

Dec. 18	Psalm 120(121) * 121(122) Gn 3:8-15, Rev 12:1-10, Jn 3:16-21
19	Psalm 122(123) * 123(124) Zep 3:14-20, Tts 1:1-16, Lk 1:1-25
20	Psalm 124(125) * 125(126), 126(127) 1Kg 2:1b-10, Tts 2:1-10, Lk 1:26-38
21	Psalm 127(128), 128(129) * 129(130), 130(131) 2Kg 7:1-17, Tts 2:11-3:8a, Lk 1:39-56
22	Psalm 131(132) * 132(133), 133(134) 2Kg 7:18-29, Gal 3:1-4, Lk 1:57-66
23	Psalm 134(135):1-7,15-21 * 135(136) Jer 38 (31):10-14, Gal 3:15-22, Lk 1:67-80

24	Psalm 136(137):1-6 * 137(138) Is 60:1-6, Gal 3:23-4:7, Mt 1:18-25

Christmas and the Week After

25	Psalm 99(100) * 94(95) Mic 4:1-5;5:2-4, 1Jn 4:7-16, Jn 3:31-36
26	Psalm 138(139) * 139(140) 2Ch. 24:17-22, Acts 6:1-7, Jn 1:1-18
27	Psalm 140(141) * 141(142) Pr 8:22-30, I Jn 5:1-12, Jn 13:20-35
28	Psalm 142(143) * 143(144) Is 49:13-23, Php 3:1-11, Mt 18:1-14
29	Psalm 144(145):1-7 * 144(145):8-21 2Kg 23:13-17b, 2Jn 1-13, Jn 2:1-11
30	Psalm 145(146) * 146(147) 3Kg 17:17-24, 3Jn 1-15, Jn 4:46-54
31	Psalm 148 * 149:1-5, 150 3Kg 3:5-14, Jam 4:13-17;5:7-11, Jn 5:1-15

The Second Week After Christmas

Jan. 1	Psalm 102(103) * 89(90) Is 62:1-5, 10-12, Rev 19:11-16, Mt 1:18-25
2	Psalm 33(34) * 32(33) 3Kg 19:1-8, Eph 4:1-16, Jn 6:1-14

3	Psalm 67(68) * 71(72) 3Kg 19:9-18, Eph 4:17-32, Jn 6:15-27
4	Psalm 84(85) * 86(87) Jos 3:14-4:7, Eph 5:1-20, Jn 9:1-12, 35-38
5	Psalm 2 * 97(98) Jon 2:2-9, Eph 6:10-20, Jn 11:17-27, 38-44
6 *Epiphany*	Psalm 148 * 149:1-5, 150 Is 49:1-7, Rev 21:22-27, Mt 12:14-21

Additional Days After Epiphany

The Psalms and Readings for the dated days after Epiphany are used only until the Sunday of the next week.

Jan.

7	Psalm 102(103) * 103(104) Dt 8:1-3, Col 1:1-14, Jn 6:30-33, 48-51
8	Psalm 116(117), 117(118) * 111(112), 112(113) Ex 17:1-7, Col 1:15-23, Jn 7:37-52
9	Psalm 120(121), 121(122), 122(123), 130(131), 131(132) Is 45:14-19, Col 1:24-2:7, Jn 8:12-19
10	Psalm 137(138), 138(139):1-17 * 146(147) Jer 23:1-8, Col 2:8-23, Jn 10:7-17
11	Psalm 148, 150 * 90(91), 91(92) Is 55:3-9, Col 3:1-17, Jn 14:6-14
12	Psalm 97(98), 98(99) * 103(104) Gn 49:1-2,8-12, Col 3:18-4:6, Jn 15:1-16

Week of First Sunday After Epiphany

Sun.	Psalm 23(24) * 18(19) Gn 1:1-2:3
Mon.	Psalm 1, 2:1-8 * 3, 4 Gn 2:4-25, Heb 1:1-14, Jn 1:1-18
Tue.	Psalm 5 * 6 Gn 3:1-24, Heb 2:1-10, Jn 1:19-28
Wed.	Psalm 7:1-11,17 * 8 Gn 4:1-16, Heb 2:11-18, Jn 1:29-42
Thu.	Psalm 9:1-10 * 9:22-39(10:1-12,16-18) Gn 4:17-26, Heb 3:1-11, Jn 1:43-51
Fri.	Psalm 10(11) * 11(12) Gn 6:1-8, Heb 3:12-19, Jn 2:1-12
Sat.	Psalm 12(13), 14(15) * 118(119):1-16 Gn 6:9-22, Heb 4:1-13, Jn 2:13-22

Use the following weekly readings until the Sunday of the Publican and the Pharisee which starts the Triodion leading to Great Lent. Consult your parish calendar for the beginning of the Triodion.

Week of the Second Sunday After Epiphany
Sunday between January 14 & 20

Sun.	Psalm 28(29) * 33(34) Gn 7:1-23
Mon.	Psalm 13(14), 15(16) * 16(17) Gn 8:6-22, Heb 4:14-5:6, Jn 2:23-3:15

Tue.	Psalm 17(18):1-16 * 17(18):17-31 Gn 9:1-17, Heb 5:7-14, Jn 3:16-21
Wed.	Psalm 18(19) * 19(20) Gn 9:18-29, Heb 6:1-12, Jn 3:22-36
Thu.	Psalm 20(21) * 22(23) Gn 11:1-9, Heb 6:13-20, Jn 4:1-15
Fri.	Psalm 21(22):1-21 * 21(22):22-31 Gn 11:27-12:8, Heb 7:1-17, Jn 4:16-26
Sat.	Psalm 23(24) * 118(119):17-32 Gn 12:9-13:1, Heb 7:18-28, Jn 4:27-42

Week of the Third Sunday After Epiphany
Sunday between January 21 & 27

Sun.	Psalm 65(66) * 45(46) Gn 13:2-18
Mon.	Psalm 24(25) * 25(26) Gn 14:1-24, Heb 8:1-13, Jn 4:43-54
Tue.	Psalm 26(27) * 27(28) Gn 15:1-11, 17-21, Heb 9:1-14, Jn 5:1-18
Wed.	Psalm 28(29) * 29(30) Gn 16:1-14, Heb 9:15-28, Jn 5:19-29
Thu.	Psalm 30(31):1-8 * 30(31):9-24 Gn 16:15-17:14, Heb 10:1-10, Jn 5:30-47
Fri.	Psalm 31(32) * 32(33) Gn 17:15-27, Heb 10:11-25, Jn 6:1-15

Sat.	Psalm 34(35):9-18 * 118(119):33-48 Gn 18:1-16, Heb 10:26-39, Jn 6:16-27

Week of the Fourth Sunday After Epiphany
Sunday between January 28 & February 3

Sun.	Psalm 92(93) * 62(63) Gn 18:16-33
Mon.	Psalm 33(34):1-10 * 33(34):11-22 Gn 19:1-29, Heb 11:1-12, Jn 6:27-40
Tue.	Psalm 35(36) * 36(37):1-11 Gn 21:1-21, Heb 11:13-22, Jn 6:41-51
Wed.	Psalm 36(37):12-29 * 36(37):30-40 Gn 22:1-18, Heb 11:23-31, Jn 6:52-59
Thu.	Psalm 37(38):1-9 * 37(38):10-22 Gn 23:1-20, Heb 11:32-12:2, Jn 6:60-71
Fri.	Psalm 38(39) * 39(40) Gn 24:1-27, Heb 12:3-11, Jn 7:1-13
Sat.	Psalm 40(41) * 118(119):49-64 Gn 24:28-38, 49-51, Heb 12:12-29, Jn 7:14-36

Week of the Fifth Sunday After Epiphany
Sunday between February 4 & 10

Sun.	Psalm 95(96) * 66(67) Gn 24:50-67
Mon.	Psalms 41(42) * 42(43) Gn 25:19-34, Heb 13:1-16, Jn 7:37-52

Tue.	Psalm 43(44):1-8 * 44(45) Gn 26:1-6, 12-33, Heb 13:17-25, Jn 7:53-8:11
Wed.	Psalm 45(46) * 46(47) Gn 27:1-29, Rom 12:1-8, Jn 8:12-20
Thu.	Psalm 47(48) * 48(49) Gn 27:30-45, Rom 12:9-21, Jn 8:21-32
Fri.	Psalm 49(50):1-15 * 50(51) Gn 27:46-28:4, 10-22, Rom 13:1-14, Jn 8:33-47
Sat.	Psalm 51(52) * 118(119):65-80 Gn 29:1-20, Rom 14:1-23, Jn 8:47-59

If more weeks are needed, turn to the week after the Week of All Saints.

Sunday of the Publican and the Pharisee
This is the beginning of the Triodion leading to Great Lent. Consult your parish calendar for this date.

Sun.	Psalm 117(118):18-29 * 97(98) Gn 29:20-35, 2Tim 3:10-15, Lk 18:10-14
Mon.	Psalm 52(53) * 53(54) Gn 30:1-24, 1Jn 1:1-10, Jn 9:1-17
Tue.	Psalm 54(55):1-8 * 55(56) Gn 31:1-24, 1Jn 2:1-11, Jn 9:18-41
Wed.	Psalm 56(57) * 60(61) Gn 31:25-50, 1Jn 2:12-17, Jn 10:1-18
Thu.	Psalm 61(62) * 62(63):1-8 Gn 32:3-21, 1Jn 2:18-29, Jn 10:19-30

Fri.	Psalm 63(64) * 64(65) Gn 32:22-33:17, 1Jn 3:1-10, Jn 10:31-42
Sat	Psalm 65(66) * 118(119):81-96 Gn 35:1-20, 1Jn 3:11-18, Jn 11:1-16

Sunday of the Prodigal Son

Sun.	Psalm 145(146) * 102(103) Pr 1:20-33, 1Co 6:12-20, Lk 15:11-32
Mon.	Psalm 66(67) * 69(70) Pr 3:11-20, 1Jn 3:18-4:6, Jn 11:17-29
Tue.	Psalm 67(68):1-18 * 67(68):24-36 Pr 4:1-27, 1Jn 4:7-21, Jn 11:30-44
Wed.	Psalm 68(69):1-13a * 68(69):13b-21, 29-36 Pr 6:1-19, 1Jn 5:1-12, Jn 11:45-54
Thu.	Psalm 70(71):1-14 * 70(71):15-24 Pr 7:1-27, 1Jn 5:13-21, Jn 11:55-12:8
Fri.	Psalm 72(73):1-14 * 72(73):15-28 Pr 8:1-21, Phm 1-25, Jn 12:9-19
Sat.	Psalm 71(72) * 118(119):97-112 Pr 8:22-35, 2Ti 1:1-14, Jn 12:20-26

Judgment Sunday (Meat-Fare Sunday)

Sun.	Psalm 146(147:1-11) * 110(111) Pr 9:1-12, 1Co 8:8-9:2, Mt 25:31-46
Mon.	Psalm 73(74):1-12 * 73(74):13-23 Pr 10:1-12, 2Ti 1:15-2:13, Jn 12:27-36a

Tue.	Psalm 74(75) * 75(76) Pr 15:16-33, 2Ti 2:14-26, Jn 12:36b-50
Wed.	Psalm 76(77) * 77(78):1-7 Pr 17:1-20, 2Ti 3:1-17, Jn 13:1-20
Thu.	Psalm 79(80) * 80(81) Pr 21:30-22:6, 2Ti 4:1-8, Jn 13:21-30
Fri.	Psalm 81(82) * 83(84) Pr 23:19-21, 29-24:2, 2Ti 4:9-22, Jn 13:31-38
Sat.	Psalm 84(85) * 118(119):113-128 Pr 25:15-28, Php 1:1-11, Jn 18:1-14

Forgiveness Sunday (Cheese-Fare Sunday)

Sun.	Psalm 147(148) * 111(112) 4Kg 2:1-12a, Rom 13:11-14:4, Mt 6:14-21
Mon.	Psalm 1, 2 * 3, 4 Pr 27:1-6, 10-12, Php 2:1-13, Jn 18:15-18, 25-27
Tue.	Psalm 5 * 6 Pr 30:1-4, 24-33, Php 3:1-11, Jn 18:28-38
Wed.	Psalm 7 * 8 Am 5:6-15, Heb. 12:1-14, Lk 18:9-14
Thu.	Psalm 9:1-10 * 9:22-39(10:1-12,16-18) Hab 3:1-19, Php 3:12-21, Jn 17:1-8
Fri.	Psalm 10(11) * 11(12) Ezk 18:1-9, 25-32, Php 4:1-9, Jn 17:9-19

Sat.	Psalm 12(13), 14(15) * 118(119):1-16 Ezk 39:21-29, Php 4:10-20, Jn 17:20-26

The First Week of Lent/The Sunday of Orthodoxy

Sun.	Psalm 23(24) * 18(19) Dan 9:3-10, Heb 11:24-26, 32-40, Jn 1:43-51
Mon.	Psalm 13(14), 15(16) * 16(17) Gn 37:1-11, 1Co 1:1-19, Mk 1:1-13
Tue.	Psalm 17(18):1-16 * 17(18):17-31 Gn 37:12-24, 1Co 1:20-31, Mk 1:14-28
Wed.	Psalm 18(19) * 19(20) Gn 37:25-36, 1Co 2:1-13, Mk 1:29-45
Thu.	Psalm 20(21):1-7 * 22(23) Gn 39:1-23, 1Co 2:14-3:15, Mk 2:1-12
Fri.	Psalm 21(22):1-21 * 21(22):22-31 Gn 40:1-23, 1Co 3:16-23, Mk 2:13-22
Sat.	Psalm 23(24) * 118(119):17-32 Gn 41:1-13, 1Co 4:1-7, Mk 2:23-3:6

The Second Week of Lent

Sun.	Psalm 28(29) * 33(34) Gn 41:14-45, Heb 1:10-2:3, Mk 2:1-12
Mon.	Psalm 24(25) * 25(26) Gn 41:46-57, 1Co 4:8-21, Mk 3:7-19a
Tue.	Psalm 26(27) * 27(28) Gn 42:1-17, 1Co 5:1-8, Mk 3:19b-35

Wed.	Psalm 28(29) * 29(30) Gn 42:18-28, 1Co 5:9-6:8, Mk 4:1-20
Thu.	Psalm 30(31):1-8 * 30(31):9-24 Gn 42:29-38, 1Co 6:12-20, Mk 4:21-34
Fri.	Psalm 31(32) * 32(33) Gn 43:1-15, 1Co 7:1-9, Mk 4:35-41
Sat.	Psalm 34(35):9-18 * 118(119):33-48 Gn 43:16-34, 1Co 7:10-24, Mk 5:1-20

The Third Week Of Lent

Sun.	Psalm 65(66) * 45(46) Gn 44:1-17, Heb 4:14-5:6, Mk 8:34-9:1
Mon.	Psalm 33(34):1-10 * 33(34):11-22 Gn 44:18-34, 1Co 7:25-31, Mk 5:21-43
Tue.	Psalm 35(36) * 36(37):1-11 Gn 45:1-15, 1Co 7:32-40, Mk 6:1-13
Wed.	Psalm 36(37):12-29 * 36(37):30-40 Gn 45:16-28, 1Co 8:1-13, Mk 6:13-29
Thu.	Psalm 37(38):1-9 * 37(38):10-22 Gn 46:1-7, 28-34, 1Co 9:1-15, Mk 6:30-46
Fri.	Psalm 38(39) * 39(40) Gn 47:1-26, 1Co 9:16-27, Mk 6:47-56
Sat.	Psalm 40(41) * 118(119):49-64 Gn 47:27-48:7, 1Co 10:1-13, Mk 7:1-23

The Fourth Week of Lent

Sun.	Psalm 92(93) * 62(63) Gn 48:8-22, Heb 6:13-20, Mk 9:17-31
Mon.	Psalm 41(42) * 42(43) Gn 49:1-28, 1Co 10:14-11:1, Mk 7:24-37
Tue.	Psalm 43(44):1-8 * 44(45) Gn 49:29-50:14, 1Co 11:17-34, Mk 8:1-10
Wed.	Psalm 45(46) * 46(47) Gn 50:15-26, 1Co 12:1-11, Mk 8:11-26
Thu.	Psalm 47(48) * 48(49) Ex 1:6-22, 1Co 12:12-26, Mk 8:27-9:1
Fri.	Psalm 49(50):1-15 * 50(51) Ex 2:1-22, 1Co 12:27-13:3, Mk 9:2-13
Sat.	Psalm 51(52) * 118(119):65-80 Ex 2:23-3:15, 1Co 13:1-13, Mk 9:14-29

The Fifth Week of Lent

Sun.	Psalm 95(96) * 66(67) Ex 3:16-4:12, Heb 9:11-14, Mk 10:32-45
Mon.	Psalm 52(53) * 53(54) Ex 4:10-31, 1Co 14:1-19, Mk 9:30-41
Tue.	Psalm 54(55):1-8 * 55(56) Ex 5:1-6:1, 1Co 14:20-33a, 39-40, Mk 9:42-50
Wed.	Psalm 56(57) * 60(61) Ex 7:8-24, 2Co 2:14-3:6, Mk 10:1-16

Thu. Psalm 61(62) * 62(63):1-8
Ex 7:25-8:19, 2Co 3:7-18, Mk 10:17-31

Fri. Psalm 63(64) * 64(65)
Ex 9:13-35, 2Co 4:1-12, Mk 10:32-45

Sat. Psalm 65(66) * 118(119):81-96
Ex 10:21-11:8, 2Co 4:13-18, Mk 10:46-52

Week of Palm Sunday

Palm Sun. Psalm 28(29) * 102(103)
Zec 9:9-12, Php 4:4-9, Jn 12:1-18

Holy Mon. Psalm 26(27) * 6
Lam 1:1-2,6-12, 2Co 1:1-7, Mk 11:12-25

Holy Tue. Psalm 30(31) * 31(32)
Lam 1:17-22, 2Co 1:8-22, Mk 12:27-33

Holy Wed. Psalm 54(55) * 142(143)
Lam 2:1-9, 2Co 1:23-2:11, Mk 12:1-11

Holy Thu. Psalm 55(56) * 63(64)
Lam 2:10-18, 1Co 10:14-17; 11:27-32
Mk 14:12-25

Holy Fri. Psalm 21(22) * 68(69)
Lam 3:1-9, 19-33, 1Pt 1:10-20, Jn 19:38-42

Holy Sat. Psalm 29(30) * 22(23)
Lam 3:37-58, Heb 4:1-16, Rom 8:1-11

Great and Holy Pascha

Easter Day	Psalm 148,149,150 * 117(118) Rom 6:3-11, Mt 28:1-20 *morning* Acts 1:1-8, Jn 1:1-17 *evening*
Mon.	Psalm 66(67) * 69(70) Ex 12:14-27, 1Co 15:1-11, Mk 16:1-8
Tue.	Psalm 67(68):1-18 * 67(68):25-36 Ex 12:28-39, 1Co 15:12-28, Mk 16:9-20
Wed.	Psalm 68(69):1-13a * 68(69):13b-21,29-36 Ex 12:40-51, 1Co 15:29-41, Mt 28:1-15
Thu.	Psalm 70(71):1-14 * 70(71):15-24 Ex 13:3-10, 1Co 15:41-50, Mt 28:16-20
Fri.	Psalm 72(73):1-14 * 72(73):15-28 Ex 13:1-2,11-16, 1Co 15:51-58, Lk 24:1-12
Sat.	Psalm 71(72) * 118(119):97-112 Ex 13:17-14:4, 2Co 4:16-5:10, Mk 12:18-27

Sunday of Saint Thomas

Sun.	Psalm 117(118):19-29 * 97(98) Ex 14:5-22, Acts 5:12-20, Jn 20:19-31
Mon.	Psalm 73(74):1-12 * 73(74):13-23 Ex 14:21-31, 1Pt 1:1-12, Jn 14:1-17
Tue.	Psalm 74(75) * 75(76) Ex 15:1-21, 1Pt 1:13-25, Jn 14:18-31

Wed.	Psalm 76(77) * 77(78):1-7 Ex 15:22-16:10, 1Pt 2:1-10, Jn 15:1-11
Thu.	Psalm 79(80) * 80(81) Ex 16:10-22, 1Pt 2:11-25, Jn 15:12-27
Fri.	Psalm 81(82) * 83(84) Ex 16:23-36, 1Pt 3:13-4:6, Jn 16:1-15
Sat.	Psalm 84(85) * 118(119):113-128 Ex 17:1-16, 1Pt 4:7-19, Jn 16:16-33

Sunday of the Myrrh-Bearers

Sun.	Psalm 145(146) * 102(103) Ex 18:1-12, Acts 6:1-7, Mk 15:43-16:8
Mon.	Psalm 85 (86) * 86 (87) Ex 18:13-27, 1Pt 5:1-14, Mt 1:1-17; 3:1-6
Tue.	Psalm 87(88) * 89(90) Ex 19:1-16, Col 1:1-14, Mt 3:7-12
Wed.	Psalm 88(89):1-18 * 88(89):19-37 Ex 19:16-25, Col 1:15-23, Mt 3:13-17
Thu.	Psalm 91(92) * 90(91) Ex 20:1-21, Col 1:24-2:7, Mt 4:1-11
Fri.	Psalm 92(93) * 93(94):14-23 Ex 24:1-18, Col 2:8-23, Mt 4:12-17
Sat.	Psalm 95(96) * 118(119):129-144 Ex 25:1-22, Col 3:1-17, Mt 4:18-25

Sunday of the Paralytic

Sun.   Psalm 146(147:1-11) * 110(111)
Ex 28:1-4, 30-38, Acts 9:32-42, Jn 5:1-15

Mon.   Psalm 96(97) * 97(98)
Ex 32:1-20, Col 3:18-4:5, Mt 5:1-10

Tue.   Psalm 98(99), 99(100) * 100(101)
Ex 32:21-34, 1Th 1:1-10, Mt 5:11-16

Wed.   Psalm 101(102):1-11 * 101(102):12-28
Ex 33:1-23, 1Th 2:1-12, Mt 5:17-20

Thu.   Psalm 102(103) * 104(105):1-15
Ex 34:1-17, 1Th 2:13-20, Mt 5:21-26

Fri.   Psalm 103(104):1-23 * 103(104):24-35
Ex 34:18-35, 1Th 3:1-13, Mt 5:27-37

Sat.   Psalm 105(106):1-8,43-48 * 118(119):145-160
Ex 40:18-32, 1Th 4:1-12, Mt 5:38-48

Sunday of the Samaritan Woman

Sun.   Psalm 147 * 111(112)
Lv 8:1-13, 30-36, Acts 11:19-30, Jn 4:5-42

Mon.   Psalm 106(107):1-16 * 106(107):17-32
Lv 16:1-19, 1Th 4:13-18, Mt 6:1-6,16-18

Tue.   Psalm 106(107):33-43 * 109(110), 110(111)
Lv 16:20-34, 1Th 5:1-11, Mt 6:7-15

Wed.   Psalm 111(112) * 112(113)
Lv 19:1-18, 1Th 5:12-28, Mt 6:19-24

Thu.	Psalm 113(114) * 114(116:1-9) Lv 19:26-37, 2Th 1:1-12, Mt 6:25-34
Fri.	Psalm 117(118):1-18 * 117(118):19-29 Lv 23:1-22, 2Th 2:1-17, Mt 7:1-12
Sat.	Psalm 115(116), 116(117) * 118(119):161-176 Lv 23:23-44, 2Th 3:1-18, Mt 7:13-21

Sunday of the Blind Man

Sun.	Psalm 149 * 114(116:10-19) Lv 25:1-17, Acts 16:16-34, John 9:1-38
Mon.	Psalm 120(121) * 121(122), 122(123) Lv 25:35-55, Col 1:9-14, Mt 13:1-16
Tue.	Psalm 123(124), 124(125) * 125(126), 126(127) Lv 26:1-20, 1Ti 2:1-6, Mt 13:18-23
Wed.	Psalm 127(128), 128(129) * 129(130), 130(131) Lv 26:27-42, Eph. 1:1-10, Mt 22:41-46
Ascension Day	Psalm 8 * 95(96) Dan 7:-14, Heb 2:5-18, Mt 28:16-20
Fri.	Psalm 134(135) * 135(136) 1Kg 2:1-10, Eph 2:1-10, Mt 7:22-27
Sat.	Psalm 136(137) * 137(138) Nm 11:16-17, 24-29, Eph 2:11-22, Mt 7:28-8:4

Sunday of the Holy Fathers

Sun.	Psalm 150 * 144(145) Wsir 43:1-12, 27-32, Acts 20:16-36 Jn 17:1-13

Mon.	Psalm 138(139) * 139(140) Jos 1:1-9, Eph 3:1-13, Mt 8:5-17
Tue.	Psalm 140(141) * 141(142) 1Kg 16:1-13a, Eph 3:14-21, Mt 8:18-27
Wed.	Psalm 142(143) * 143(144) Is 4:2-6, Eph 4:1-16, Mt 8:28-34
Thu.	Psalm 144(145):1-7 * 144(145):8-21 Zec 4:1-14, Eph 4:17-32, Mt 9:1-8
Fri.	Psalm 145(146) * 146(147) Jer 38(31):31-34, Eph 5:1-20, Mt 9:9-17
Sat.	Psalm 148 * 149:1-5,150 Ezk 36:22-27, Eph 6:10-24, Mt 9:18-26

Pentecost

Pentecost	Psalm 117(118) * 144(145) Dt. 16:9-12, Acts 2:1-9, Jn 7:37-52, 8:12
Mon.	Psalm 52(53) * 53(54) Ezk 33:1-11, 1Jn 1:1-10, Mt 9:27-34
Tue.	Psalm 54(55):1-8 * 55(56) Ezk 33:21-31, 1Jn 2:1-11, Mt 9:35-10:4
Wed.	Psalm 56(57) * 60(61) Ezk 34:1-16, 1 Jn 2:12-17, Mt 10:5-15
Thu.	Psalm 61(62) * 62(63):1-8 Ezk 37:15-28, 1Jn 2:18-29, Mt 10:16-23

Fri.	Psalm 63(64) * 64(65) Ezk 39:21-29, 1Jn 3:1-10, Mt 10:24-33
Sat	Psalm 65(66) * 118(119):81-96 Ezk 47:1-12, 1Jn 3:11-18, Mt 10:34-42

Sunday of All Saints

Sun.	Psalm 146 * 147 Pr 3:11-20, Heb 11:33-12:2 Mt 10:32-33, 37-38; 19:27-30
Mon.	Psalm 66(67) * 69(70) Pr 3:23-38, 1Jn 3:18-24, Mt 11:1-6
Tue.	Psalm 67(68):1-18 * 67(68):24-35 Pr 4:1-27, 1Jn 4:7-21, Mt 11:7-15
Wed.	Psalm 68(69):1-13a * 68(69):13b-21, 29-36 Pr 6:1-19, 1Jn 5:1-12, Mt 11:16-24
Thu.	Psalm 70(71):1-14 * 70(71):15-24 Pr 7:1-27, 1Jn 5:13-21, Mt 11:25-30
Fri.	Psalm 72(73):1-14 * 72(73):15-28 Pr 8:1-21, 2Jn 1-13, Mt 12:1-14
Sat.	Psalm 71(72) * 118(119):97-112 Pr 8:22-35, 3Jn 1-15, Mt 12:15-21

After finishing the week of All Saints, look down in the next few weekly readings until you find the one corresponding to the next Sunday on the calendar.

3rd Sunday — Week of the Sunday closest to May 25

- **Sun.** Psalm 146(147:1-11) * 110(111)
  Pr 9:1-12

- **Mon.** Psalm 73(74):1-12 * 73(74):13-23
  Pr 10:1-12, 1Ti 1:1-17, Mt 12:22-32

- **Tue.** Psalm 74(75) * 75(76)
  Pr 15:16-33, 1Ti 1:18-2:8, Mt 12:33-42

- **Wed.** Psalm 76(77) * 77(78):1-7
  Pr 17:1-20, 1Ti 3:1-16, Mt 12:43-50

- **Thu.** Psalm 79(80) * 80(81)
  Pr 21:30-22:6, 1Ti 4:1-16, Mt 13:24-30

- **Fri.** Psalm 81(82) * 83(84)
  Pr 23:19-21, 29-24:2, 1Ti 5:17-25, Mt 13:31-35

- **Sat.** Psalm 84(85) * 118(119):113-128
  Pr 25:15-28, 1Ti 6:6-21, Mt 13:36-43

4th Sunday — Week of the Sunday closest to June 1

- **Sun.** Psalm 23(24) * 18(19)
  Ecc 1:1-11

- **Mon.** Psalm 85 (86) * 86 (87)
  Ecc 2:1-15, Gal 1:1-17, Mt 13:44-52

- **Tue.** Psalm 87(88) * 89(90)
  Ecc 2:16-26, Gal 1:18-2:10, Mt 13:53-58

Wed.	Psalm 88(89):1-18 * 88(89):19-37 Ecc 3:1-15, Gal 2:11-21, Mt 14:1-12
Thu.	Psalm 91(92) * 89(91) Ecc 3:16-4:3, Gal 3:1-14, Mt 14:13-21
Fri.	Psalm 92(93) * 93(94):14-23 Ecc 5:1-7, Gal 3:15-22, Mt 14:22-36
Sat.	Psalm 95(96) * 118(119):129-144 Ecc 5:8-20, Gal 3:23-4:11, Mt 15:1-20
5th Sunday	**Week of the Sunday closest to June 8**
Sun.	Psalm 28(29) * 33(34) Ecc 6:1-12
Mon.	Psalm 96(97) * 97(98) Ecc 7:1-14, Gal 4:12-20, Mt 15:21-28
Tue.	Psalm 98(99), 99(100) * 100(101) Ecc 8:14-9:10, Gal 4:21-31, Mt 15:29-39
Wed.	Psalm 101(102):1-11 * 101(102):12-28 Ecc 9:11-18, Gal 5:1-15, Mt 16:1-12
Thu.	Psalm 102(103) * 104(105):1-15 Ecc 11:1-8, Gal 5:16-24, Mt 16:13-20
Fri.	Psalm 103(104):1-23 * 103(104):24-35 Ecc 11:9-12:14, Gal 5:25-6:10, Mt 16:21-28
Sat.	Psalm 105(106):1-8, 43-48 * 118(119):145-160 Nm 3:1-13, Gal 6:11-18, Mt 17:1-13

6th Sunday   **Week of the Sunday closest to June 15**

Sun.   Psalm 65(66) * 45(46)
         Nm 6:22-26

Mon.   Psalm 106(107):1-16 * 106(107):17-32
         Nm 9:15-23; 10:29-36, Rom 1:1-15
         Mt 17:14-21

Tue.   Psalm 106(107):33-43 * 109(110), 110(111)
         Nm 11:1-23, Rom 1:16-25, Mt 17:22-27

Wed.   Psalm 111(112) * 112(113)
         Nm 11:24-35, Rom 1:28-2:11, Mt 18:1-9

Thu.   Psalm 113(114) * 114(115)
         Nm 12:1-16, Rom 2:12-24, Mt 18:10-20

Fri.   Psalm 117(118):1-18 * 117(118):19-29
         Nm 13:1-3, 21-30, Rom 2:25-3:8, Mt 18:21-35

Sat.   Psalm 115(116), 116(117) * 118(119):161-176
         Nm 13:31-14:25, Rom 3:9-20, Mt 19:1-12

7th Sunday   **Week of the Sunday closest to June 22**

Sun.   Psalm 92(93) * 62(63)
         Nm 14:26-45

Mon.   Psalm 120(121) * 121(122), 122(123)
         Nm 16:1-19, Rom 3:21-31, Mt 19:13-22

Tue.   Psalm 123(124), 124(125) * 129(130), 130(131)
         Nm 16:20-35, Rom 4:1-12, Mt 19:23-30

Wed.	Psalm 127(128), 128(129) * 129(130), 130(131) Nm 17:16-28, Rom 4:13-25, Mt 20:1-16
Thu.	Psalm 131(132) * 132(133), 133(134) Nm 18:1-14, Rom 5:1-11, Mt 20:17-28
Fri.	Psalm 134(135):1-7, 15-21 * 135(136) Nm 20:1-13, Rom 5:12-21, Mt 20:29-34
Sat.	Psalm 136(137):1-6 * 127(128) Nm 20:14-29, Rom 6:1-11, Mt 21:1-11
8*th* Sunday	Week of the Sunday closest to June 29
Sun.	Psalm 92(93) * 62(63) Nm 21:4-9, 21-35
Mon.	Psalm 138(139) * 139(140) Nm 22:1-21, Rom 6:12-23, Mt 21:12-22
Tue.	Psalm 140(141) * 141(142) Nm 22:21-38, Rom 7:1-12, Mt 21:23-32
Wed.	Psalm 142(143) * 143(144) Nm 22:41-23:12, Rom 7:13-25, Mt 21:33-46
Thu.	Psalm 144(145):1-7 * 144(145):8-21 Nm 23:11-26, Rom 8:1-11, Mt 22:1-14
Fri.	Psalm 145(146) * 146(147) Nm 24:1-13, Rom 8:12-17, Mt 22:15-22
Sat.	Psalm 147(148) * 148(149):1-5, 150 Nm 24:12-25, Rom 8:18-25, Mt 22:23-40

9th Sunday   **Week of the Sunday closest to July 6**

Sun.   Psalm 95(96) * 66(67)
Nm 27:12-23

Mon.   Psalm 1, 2:1-8 * 3, 4
Nm 32:1-6, 16-27, Rom 8:26-30, Mt 23:1-12

Tue.   Psalm 5 * 6
Nm 35:1-3, 9-15, 30-34, Rom 8:31-39
Mt 23:13-26

Wed.   Psalm 7 * 8
Dt. 1:1-18, Rom 9:1-18, Mt 23:27-39

Thu.   Psalm 9:1-10 * 9:21-39 (10:1-12, 16-18)
Dt. 3:18-28, Rom 9:19-33, Mt 24:1-14

Fri.   Psalm 10(11) * 11(12)
Dt. 31:7-13, 24-32:4, Rom 10:1-13
Mt 24:15-31

Sat.   Psalm 12(13), 14(15) * 118(119):1-16
Dt. 34:1-12, Rom 10:14-21, Mt 24:32-51

10th Sunday   **Week of the Sunday closest to July 13**

Sun.   Psalm 117(118):19-29 * 97(98)
Jos 1:1-18

Mon.   Psalm 13(14), 15(16) * 16(17)
Jos 2:1-14, Rom 11:1-12, Mt 25:1-13

Tue.   Psalm 17(18):1-16 * 17(18):17-31
Jos 2:15-24, Rom 11:13-24, Mt 25:14-30

Wed.	Psalm 18(19) * 19(20) Jos 3:1-13, Rom 11:25-36, Mt 25:31-46
Thu.	Psalm 20(21):1-7 * 22(23) Jos 3:14-4:7, Rom 12:1-8, Mt 26:1-16
Fri.	Psalm 21(22):1-21 * 21(22):22-31 Jos 4:19-5:1, 10-15, Rom 12:9-21, Mt 26:17-25
Sat.	Psalm 23(24) * 118(119):17-32 Jos 6:1-14, Rom 13:1-7, Mt 26:26-35

11th Sunday   *Week of the Sunday closest to July 20*

Sun.	Psalm 145(146) * 102(103) Jos 6:15-27
Mon.	Psalm 24(25) * 25(26) Jos 7:1-13, Rom 13:8-14, Mt 26:36-46
Tue.	Psalm 26(27) * 27(28) Jos 8:22-29, Rom 14:1-12, Mt 26:47-56
Wed.	Psalm 28(29) * 29(30) Jos 8:30-35, Rom 14:13-23, Mt 26:57-68
Thu.	Psalm 30(31):1-8 * 30(31):9-24 Jos 9:3-21, Rom 15:1-13, Mt 26:69-75
Fri.	Psalm 31(32) * 32(33) Jos 9:22-10:15, Rom 15:14-24, Mt 27:1-10
Sat.	Psalm 34(35):9-18 * 118(119):33-48 Jos 23:1-16, Rom 15:25-33, Mt 27:11-23

12th **Sunday**   **Week of the Sunday closest to July 27**

Sun.   Psalm 99(100) * 101(102):19-29
           Jos 24:1-15

Mon.   Psalm 33(34):1-10 * 33(34):11-22
           Jos 24:16-33, Rom 16:1-16, Mt 27:24-31

Tue.   Psalms 35(36) * 36(37):1-11
           Jdg 2:1-5, 11-23, Rom 16:17-27, Mt 27:32-44

Wed.   Psalm 36(37):12-29 * 36(37):30-40
           Jdg 3:12-30, Acts 1:1-14, Mt 27:45-54

Thu.   Psalm 37(38):1-9 * 37(38):10-22
           Jdg 4:4-23, Acts 1:15-26, Mt 27:55-66

Fri.   Psalm 38(39) * 39(40)
           Jdg 5:1-18, Acts 2:1-21, Mt 28:1-10

Sat.   Psalm 40(41) * 118(119):49-64
           Jdg 5:19-31, Acts 2:22-36, Mt 28:11-20

13th **Sunday**   **Week of the Sunday closest to August 3**

Sun.   Psalm 147(148) * 111(112)
           Jdg 6:1-24

Mon.   Psalm 41(42) * 42(43)
           Jdg 6:25-40, Acts 2:37-47, Jn 1:1-18

Tue.   Psalm 43(44):1-8 * 44(45)
           Jdg 7:1-18, Acts 3:1-11, Jn 1:19-28

Wed.   Psalm 45(46) * 46(47)
           Jdg 7:19-8:12, Acts 3:12-26, Jn 1:29-42

Thu.	Psalm 47(48) * 48(49) Jdg 8:22-35, Acts 4:1-12, Jn 1:43-51
Fri.	Psalm 49(50):1-15 * 50(51) Jdg 9:1-21, Acts 4:13-31, Jn 2:1-12
Sat.	Psalm 51(52) * 118(119):65-80 Jdg 9:22-25, 50-57, Acts 4:32-5:11, Jn 2:13-25

14th Sunday *Week of the Sunday closest to August 10*

Sun.	Psalm 149 * 114(116:1-9) Jdg 11:1-11, 29-39
Mon.	Psalm 52(53) * 53(54) Jdg 12:1-7, Acts 5:12-26, Jn 3:1-21
Tue.	Psalm 54(55):1-8 * 55(56) Jdg 13:1-15, Acts 5:27-42, Jn 3:22-36
Wed.	Psalm 56(57) * 60(61) Jdg 13:15-24, Acts 6:1-15a, Jn 4:1-26
Thu.	Psalm 61(62) * 62(63):1-8 Jdg 14:1-19, Acts 7:1-16, Jn 4:27-42
Fri.	Psalm 63(64) * 64(65) Jdg 14:20-15:20, Acts 7:17-29, Jn 4:43-54
Sat.	Psalm 65(66) * 118(119):81-96 Jdg 16:1-14, Acts 7:30-43, Jn 5:1-18

15th Sunday *Week of the Sunday closest to August 17*

Sun.	Psalm 150 * 144(145) Jdg 16:15-31

Mon.	Psalm 66(67) * 69(70) Jdg 17:1-13, Acts 7:44-8:1a, Jn 5:19-29
Tue.	Psalm 67(68):1-18 * 67(68):24-35 Jdg 18:1-15, Acts 8:1-13, Jn 5:30-47
Wed.	Psalm 68(69):1-13a * 68(69):13b-21,29-36 Jdg 18:16-31, Acts 8:14-25, Jn 6:1-15
Thu.	Psalm 70(71):1-14 * 70(71):15-24 Job 1:1-22, Acts 8:26-40, Jn 6:16-27
Fri.	Psalm 72(73):1-14 * 72(73):15-28 Job 2:1-15, Acts 9:1-9, Jn 6:28-40
Sat.	Psalm 71(72) * 118(119):97-112 Job 3:1-26, Acts 9:10-19a, Jn 6:41-51

16th Sunday   **Week of the Sunday closest to August 24**

Sun.	Psalm 23(24) * 18(19) Job 4:1-6, 12-21
Mon.	Psalm 73(74):1-12, 73(74):13-23 Job 4:1; 5:1-11, 17-21, 26-27, Acts 9:19b-31 Jn 6:52-59
Tue.	Psalm 74(75) * 75(76) Job 6:1-4, 8-15, 21, Acts 9:32-43, Jn 6:60-71
Wed.	Psalm 76(77) * 77(78):1-7 Job 6:1; 7:1-21, Acts 10:1-16, Jn 7:1-13
Thu.	Psalm 79(80) * 80(81) Job 8:1-10, 20-22, Acts 10:17-33, Jn 7:14-36

Fri. Psalm 81(82) * 83(84)
Job 9:1-15, 32-35, Acts 10:34-48, Jn 7:37-52

Sat. Psalm 84(85) * 118(119):113-128
Job 9:1; 10:1-9, 16-22, Acts 11:1-18
Jn 8:12-20

Sources and Acknowledgments

Sincere gratitude is extended to the men and woman who, through the moving of God's Spirit, produced the materials and sources for this book. Gratitude is also extended to the publishers and owners of copyrights who gave their permission to use these materials

A sincere effort has been made to identify all the sources used for the preparation of this work; but because of the nature of prayer and the language of worship, phrases and thoughts often become common by usage. Sources that have been overlooked will be gratefully acknowledged.

Recommended Bibles

Please consult your priest for his recommendations as to what Bible to read.

The Orthodox Study Bible, copyright 2008 by St. Athanasius Academy of Orthodox Theology, Thomas Nelson publishers. This study bible uses the New King James version (as the NT text), and includes material about Orthodoxy. Some of the footnote comments in the Old Testament section prefigure Jesus Christ too quickly, and do not indicate the unfolding of revelation

The New Oxford Annotated Bible with the Apocrypha, copyright 1977 by Oxford University Press, Inc., New York. This bible uses the Revised Standard Version, and the notes reflect Protestant and Catholic scholarship during the period when it was published.

Sources For Prayer and Study

The following is a list of prayer books and prayer resources you may wish to consult or use in daily prayer. Your priest may have other recommendations.

My Orthodox Prayer Book, by Fr. Theodore G. Stylianopoulos, Greek Orthodox Archdiocese of America, Department of Religious Education, Brookline, MA, 1985, revised 2011.

Speaking to God, by Archbishop Demetrios, Greek Orthodox Archdiocese of America, NY, 2012.

Beginning to Pray, by Archbishop Anthony Bloom, Paulist Press, NY, 1970.

The Year of Grace of the Lord, by A Monk of the Eastern Church, St. Vladimir's Seminary Press, Crestwood, NY, 1980.

The Prologue of Ohrid, by Saint Nikolai Velimirovic, Sebastian Press, Western American Diocese, 2008, Vol. I & II.

A Prayer Book for Orthodox Christians, translated from the Greek by the Holy Transfiguration Monastery, Boston, MA, 2009.

A Manual of the Hours of the Orthodox Church, compiled by Archimandrite Cherubim, Holy Myrrhbearers Monastery, Otego, NY, 1998.

Praying with the Orthodox Tradition, compiled by Stefano Parenti, St. Vladimir's Seminary Press, Crestwood, NY, 1996.

Daily Prayers for Orthodox Christians, The Synekdemos, Edited by N. Michael Vaporis, Holy Cross Orthodox Press, Brookline, MA, 2010.

Other Sources Used Or Quoted In This Book

Quotations from the Revised Standard Version of the Bible, copyrighted 1946 and 1952 by the Division of Christian Education of the National Council of the Churches of Christ in the United States of America.

The Kathisma Psalter with the Nine Canticles Revised According to the Septuagint, Prepared by Holy Myrrhbearers Monastery, Otego, NY, 2005.

The Book of Common Prayer, copyright 1979 by Charles Mortimer Guilbert as Custodian of the Standard Book of Common Prayer.

The Daily Office, copyright 1968, The Joint Liturgical Group; published by S.P.C.K. and the Epworth Press.

Lutheran Book of Worship, copyright 1978 by the Lutheran Church in America, The American Lutheran Church, The Evangelical Lutheran Church of Canada, and the Lutheran Church Missouri Synod.

The Book of Common Worship, copyright, 1946, by The Board of Christian Education of the Presbyterian Church in the United States of America; renewed 1974.

Acknowledgments

Punctuation has been altered in the following sources:

pp. 17-18, 44-46, 69 adapted from *The Synekdemos* pp. 17, 18, 51, 52.

p. 18 "Lord God our heavenly Father..." from *The Book of Common Prayer,* p. 137, alt.

p.18-24ff. Psalm 83(84), 61(62), 94(95), 8, 120(121), 62(63), 89(90), from *The New Oxford Annotated Bible,* pp. 660, passim.

p. 47 & 48, Psalm 50(51) from *The Kathisma Psalter,* pp. 49-50.

pp. 71 & 72 from *The Synekdemos,* pp. 1-2.

p. 86 "Lord Jesus be our..." from *The Book of Common Worship,* p. 374, alt.

pp. 89-91 *The Orthodox Study Bible,* p. vii.

pp. 24-43 & 49-68 *Intercessions (pp. 24-43) and Thanksgivings (pp. 49-68)* modeled on T*he Daily Office,* pp. 90-97 alt.

pp. 93-163 *Daily Bible Readings--Year 1 (pp. 93-127) and Year 2 (pp. 129-163),* contains psalms from *The Daily Office,* pp. 33-35; readings from *The Book of Common Prayer,* pp. 889-995; and **Lutheran Book of Worship,** pp. 179-192. The material has been altered to fit the Orthodox calendar.

www.ingramcontent.com/pod-product-compliance
Lightning Source LLC
Chambersburg PA
CBHW061309110426
42742CB00012BA/2119